THE GOD I DON'T BELIEVE IN:

CHARTING A NEW COURSE FOR CHRISTIANITY

To Bev . . .
My True Soulmate

THE GOD I DON'T BELIEVE IN:

CHARTING A NEW COURSE FOR CHRISTIANITY

GARY ALAN WILBURN

PROGRESSIVE PUB

Stamford, CT

ISBN: 978-0-9701374-1-8

ProgressivePub
Stamford, CT
For information e-mail contactus@ProgressivePub.com

Cover design by Sean Wilburn,
sean@wilburnconsulting.com

Book design by Cheryl Mirkin,
CMF Graphic Design

Printed in the United States of America.

CONTENTS

ACKNOWLEDGEMENTS

I am deeply grateful to my very good friends Meyrick and Donna Payne and Gail Linstrom, for their unending friendship and editorial assistance in bringing this book to life. And a special thanks to my son, Sean Wilburn, without whose inquiring mind and technological expertise none of these thoughts would have seen the light of day. And finally to Cheryl Mirkin of CMF Graphic Design who so expeditiously and graciously met an extremely ambitious publication schedule.

I also wish to express appreciation to the hundreds of restless and searching young people and adults who have travelled this road of determination and discovery with me over the past 25 years. These are friends and colleagues from the Bel Air Presbyterian Church and Immanuel Presbyterian Church in Los Angeles, California, as well as the First Presbyterian Church of Stamford, Connecticut, and most recently the First Presbyterian Church of New Canaan, Connecticut.

66 There are literally dozens of well known theologians and biblical scholars who have written hundreds of books challenging Christians to rethink what they mean by Christianity. Usually they write these books in their secluded studies and their private offices. But it is a rare delight when a pastor in the trenches can write such an open and informative book about a journey, through study and interaction with members of his congregation that changed his vision of the Christian path. This is a wonderful book for any individual who is trying to figure out why they are no longer comfortable with the Christianity of their youth, and are searching for a new way to think, and talk about their faith. It is also great resource for those in small groups who want to explore the roots of their faith together. And finally this book can serve as a model for other clergy who are trying to lead their congregations into the 21st century. **99**

—FRED C. PLUMER
President, The Center for Progressive Christianity

PREFACE

*"The potential of the average person
is like a huge ocean unsailed,
a new continent unexplored,
a world of possibilities waiting to be released
and channeled toward some great good."*
—TRACY BRIAN

In an essay in the *New York Times*, screenwriter Marty Kaplan speaks for today's generation: "The boomers wrestling with their interfaith marriages, their children's questions about the Creator, their friends' cancers, their own mortality—where are the troubled [skeptics] turning now? Too stable to be seduced by cults, too secular to be born again, too pained to ignore our unease, we have become a generation of seekers, searching for something transcendent to fill the hole where God was."[1]

Having spent much of my life working with students, skeptics, and seekers on the West and East Coasts, I agree wholeheartedly with Kaplan. I am honored when a thoughtful person has the integrity to tell me, "I don't believe in God!" Rather than dismissing it as tacit unbelief, I often respond, "Really . . . tell me about the God you don't believe in."

When I listen to their stories, each of them unique, it is not long before I find myself saying, "You know what? I don't believe in that God either!" At that moment the mystery of life begins to unfold for both of us.

In his recent book, *Without God, Without Creed, the Origins of*

Unbelief in America, James Turner makes a startling but accurate observation. "Unbelief was not something that 'happened' to religion," he says. "On the contrary, religion caused unbelief."[2]

I recently counseled a young couple about their upcoming marriage. He is a convinced fundamentalist Christian, and she a convinced secular humanist. "I don't believe in God," she told me. They are good kids. They love each other. They share a number of things in common. The only potential obstacle to their future happiness together is that, even though he thinks his fiancée is a truly good person, he truly believes that when she dies she is going to go to hell for all eternity because she has not "accepted Jesus Christ as her personal Lord and Savior." As he sat in my office holding hands with his fiancé, he said, "I hate to think of my wife going to hell, but I didn't make up the rules. God did in the Bible."

I don't believe in that God.

Not long ago, I had a brief conversation with two young, intelligent women whose spiritual quest led them to a Women's Bible Study group in which, as they put it, they can "study God's Word directly as it came from God, without any other philosophies or man-made thoughts getting in the way." "It's so great!" they told me. "We don't need any scholars or theologians telling us what the Bible means. We just pray and read the Bible as it was written by God, and God teaches us the truth."

It was neither the time nor place to explore the field of Biblical Studies or the History of Religions with them, but I wondered if God would lead them to follow the Biblical commands in Leviticus to kill their disobedient children or stone to death adulterous wives or sell them into sex-slavery, or to follow St. Paul's commandments of apartheid in the New Testament that slaves must be obedient to their masters, or that women should be silent in church and not teach men, but rather ask their husbands any questions they might have about religion and the Scriptures at home.

I don't believe in that God.

Hundreds of preachers in supposedly Christian Churches

throughout America have cast blame for the devastation of Hurricane Katrina on what they declare are the godless lives of Creoles, Muslims, gays, lesbians, witches, evolutionists, liberals, Democrats, musicians, the poor, and the homeless. They firmly believe that God caused Katrina as an act of divine judgment.

I don't believe in that God.

Many in our government's current administration are talking publicly these days about "The American Empire," and are acting with unprecedented and unbridled power and authority under what appears to be a divine mandate of world-dominance reminiscent of ancient Rome under the Caesars.

I don't believe in that God.

When George W. Bush was asked recently about the role that faith has played in his presidency, he replied, "I don't see how you can be President . . . without a relationship with the Lord." I believe he was deeply sincere. And God knows our leaders need all the help they can get. But that language of intimacy with the Almighty from an evangelical Christian who claims divine support for his "Godly mission" causes some of us to be scared to death about the assumption that America is a Christian nation that only Christians should govern.

I don't believe in that God.

In our global-village world, with America's stockpiles of nuclear weapons already able to kill everything on earth several times over, there are those in the present administration and around the world who are calling for increased nuclear weapon production and relaxed rules of deployment "in the Name of God."

I don't believe in that God.

A friend recently said to me, "Gary, I don't know how a non-Christian could live in today's world without the certainty of heaven that Christianity provides for us. If Jesus didn't come to earth to die for our sins to forgive us so that we can live forever, I don't know how I could go on living. What's the point of living if you're not a Christian and this screwed-up world is all there is?"

I don't believe in that God.

If you don't either, there is another option: to open yourself self to an emerging faith which finds more grace in the search for meaning than in absolute certainty, and more life in the questions than in the answers. As Galileo said 400 years ago, *"I do not feel obliged to believe that the same God who has endowed us with sense, reason, and intellect has intended us to forgo their use."*

That's the God I believe in. I invite you to join me in the journey.

For some years now I have led expanding congregations of progressive Christians in discovering a new vitality in our spiritual quest. We describe ourselves as "a thinking person's church." We believe in thinking and want to think in believing. We enjoy the challenge of worshipping God with our minds, not just our hearts. We believe that all of life's big questions are spiritual, and while there are no easy answers, we seek to provide a safe, open, and inclusive forum in which to explore them.

When I hear language like "You can't be saved unless you accept Christ as your personal savior," I know that it is usually sincere and heart-felt. But what it most likely means is, "We are on the inside, and you are on the outside. Ours is the only true faith. If you do it our way, you'll have better access to God than the followers of Moses or Buddha or Mohammed, or Charles Darwin, or the 'Inner Light,' or whatever. We welcome everyone into God's family . . . as long as you're willing to become like us."

That kind of insular theology makes Christianity a religion of exclusion, not inclusion—a far cry from the universality of Abraham, through whom God promised the blessing of all the nations of the earth, and of which Paul spoke when he said, "We have our hope set on the living God, who is the savior of all people, especially of those who believe."[3]

As a progressive Christian, I see in Jesus the true image and likeness of God. For me, Jesus is the face of God, the heart of God, the ethics of God, the way of God. In Jesus I am discovering what a life full of God looks like. As a follower of Jesus, I unapologetically proclaim Jesus Christ as my access into the realm of God. But at the same time, I recognize the faithfulness of many other people who have other names for their access into God's realm.[4]

There are many of us today who are working to make our separate communities of faith places of free inquiry and spiritual discovery for all people—places for those who have neither abandoned the faith nor sought refuge in a narrow version of it. We seek to deepen our commitment to the truth of our Christian tradition while at the same time discovering, respecting, perhaps even reverencing, and integrating the truth of others' traditions. Because, at the end of the day, we believe that God is bigger than any of our ideas about God.

Ours is not the easy road of simply believing a set of ancient creeds or politically correct doctrinal statements. According to the gospels, Jesus did not bring us a new religion or a new code of ethics. What he brought us was a life filled with God, acting as God would act. Rarely did he give a straight answer to a straight question. Instead he responded with another question, or told a puzzling story. Jesus put his questioners in a position of having to think for themselves. Rather than offer simple answers to life's most perplexing problems, Jesus heightened the ambiguity. As much as we might want him to be so, Jesus was not a "black and white" kind of guy. He knew what we are still discovering, that absolute answers lead to false confidence and security and become substitutes for God.

As my friend and mentor, William Sloane Coffin, would often say, "It is a mistake to look to the Bible to close a discussion; the Bible seeks to open one. God leads with a light rein, giving us our head . . . . Christians have to listen to the World as well as to the Word—to science, to history, to what reason and our own experience tell us. We do not honor the higher truth we find in Christ by ignoring truths found elsewhere."[5]

Many of us today call ourselves "progressive Christians." By that we simply mean that we are attempting to embrace the essential teachings of Jesus—the heart of which is Jesus' love for all people, his vision for a just society, and his compassionate inclusion and treatment of people who are generally excluded from society. I like the sign that Jim Adams posted outside his church in Washington, D.C.: *"Curious Pagans and Bored Christians Are Welcome!"*

My brother Thom died unexpectedly early in 2007. In what was to be his final e-mail to me, he signed off with this: *"A mind that has been stretched will never return to its original dimension!"* I believe that to be true for the heart as well.

I invite you to join with a growing number of us around the world who are attempting to chart a new course for Christianity. Our journey has three destinations:

A Faith Beyond Creeds . . .
A Humanity Beyond Borders . . . and
A World Beyond War.

Like any sea journey, there are great adventures and dangerous hidden shoals along the way. But there are also great discoveries and wonderful transformations. *The rougher the sea the stronger the character.* It is of this journey that I write in the pages to follow. I also solicit your own thoughts on this undertaking. I can be reached by e-mail at Gary.Wilburn@ProgressivePub.com.

Gary Alan Wilburn

A FAITH
BEYOND CREEDS

CHAPTER 1

POSITIONING OUR SAILS TO THE WIND

"It is time we steered by the stars,
not by the lights of each passing ship."
—GENERAL OMAR BRADLEY

Early in the last century, in the days when the great fleets of ships went out of New Bedford, Massachusetts, to scour the oceans of the world, the most famous skipper of them all was Eleazar Hull. Captain Hull took his vessel into more remote seas, pushed the limits farther, brought home more bounty, and lost fewer crewman in the process than any other captain of his time. This was all the more remarkable since he had no formal navigational training.

When asked how he guided his ship so infallibly over the trackless seas, he would reply: "Well, when the skies are clear at dusk, I go up on deck, rock slowly with the pitch and roll of my ship, listen to the wind in the riggin', get the drift of the sea, and take a long look at the stars. Then I'd set my course."

One day, however, the march of time caught up with this ancient mariner. The fleet's insurance underwriters from Boston insisted that all ship captains be required to attend Harvard College for advanced training in the science of navigation. Three of the company's top executives met with Captain Hull and told him that he must either go back to school or retire.

To their amazement, the old fellow responded enthusiastically. He had, it appeared, always wanted to know something about "science," and he was entirely willing to spend several months studying it, especially at company expense. So the arrangements were made. Eleazar Hull went to school, studied hard, and graduated near the top of his class. Then he returned to his ship, set out to sea, and was gone for two years.

When he returned to the dock he was met by the company's officers and members of the board. They asked him how it felt to navigate by the book, after so many years of doing it the other way. "It was wonderful," Captain Hull replied with a grin. Whenever I wanted to know my position, I'd go down into my cabin, get out all the charts, work through the proper equations, and set a course with mathematical precision. Then I'd go up on deck, rock slowly with the pitch and roll of my ship, listen to the wind in the riggin', get the drift of the sea, and take a long look at the stars. And correct my computations for error!"[6]

Well, let's face it: We are all children of the Enlightenment. We take our rationality very seriously. As well we should. But let's be honest. Most of us, as Bill Coffin put it, "tend to hold certainty dearer than truth. We want to learn only what we already know. We want to become only what we already are."[7] In any other age that position may have served us well. But today's world calls for a reassessment of all of our past assumptions.

We are in pretty rough seas these days—around the globe, in our nation, in our families, and in our warring faith communities. No sooner do we finish mapping a course for our lives than the fixed boundaries of our faith and worldview change, like old maps of Russia or Palestine, and we are forced back to our drawing boards. The scientific, theological, moral, and ethical decks on which we once stood are trembling under foot, as if from some great seismic shift in the ocean's tectonic plate. We know that we cannot weather the storm alone, but we are too fearful and suspicious of one another to stand together.

How does one know where to stand, and how to keep one's balance in today's rapidly changing world—especially in this old ship we call Christianity, or the Church, or religion in general? It is pretty crowded with all of us down in the hold—and awfully loud. There is too much heat and not enough light. And there are no longer enough private compartments to keep some of us from killing the rest of us. Fights break out regularly around the mess table. Little mutinies rise up all too often. And not a few of the crew have already jumped ship.

All the while our mainline churches, the previous standard-bearers of our religion, are losing numerical strength, public hearing, and persuasive power for good year after year. Each port we stop at we take on another team of "experts" to do some soundings for us and publish another report. We have more reports than members! It does not take a rocket scientist to tell us that our church pews are emptier than ever and our denominational bureaucracies are more focused on self-preservation than on advancing the good news of our faith.

The fact is our religious ships are dead in the water. The answer is not bigger and better sails. It is how we "listen to the wind in the riggin'" and how we position our sails to the wind.

If anything is going to change, we need to take personal responsibility for our own spiritual voyage, be we young or old, women or men, gay or straight, comfortable or struggling, conservative or progressive of whatever religion, race, creed, or gender. As Dr. Martin Luther King said, "We are all a great world house." We can no longer survive independently from one another. We need to rise up out of the stifling confinement of our narrow cubicles and the oppressive confines of the ship's hold and stand together on the deck. Then, together, we shall once again breathe deeply the fresh wind of God's Spirit.

Our rights and entitlements, our creedal statements, our historic interpretations, traditional distinctives, and bureaucratic structures have outlived their usefulness. Our fragile planet is at the mercy of our ancient world views, our inflexible orthodoxies, our private greed, and our "warring madness."

Assuming that you have come to this point in the journey with your own preconceptions in mind, your own charts in hand, your own proper equations worked out, and possibly your own course already set with mathematical precision, I invite you to come up on deck with an increasing number of us, breathe deeply, rock slowly with the pitch and roll of the ship, listen to the wind in the riggin', get the drift of the sea, and take a long look at the stars. And then quite possibly, as I have, "correct your computations for error."

I cannot imagine a better blessing on our voyage than this:

*"May God give you
grace never to sell yourself short,
grace to risk something big for something good, and
grace to remember that the world is now
too dangerous for anything but truth and
too small for anything but love."*[8]

Let the voyage begin...

CHAPTER 2

LEAVING OUR OUTGROWN SHELLS

Build thee more stately

mansions, O my soul.

As the swift seasons roll,

Leave thy low-vaulted past.

Let each new temple,

nobler than the last,

Shut thee from heaven

with a dome more vast,

'till thou at length art free,

Leaving thine outgrown shell,

by life's unresting sea.

— OLIVER WENDELL HOLMES,
"THE CHAMBERED NAUTILUS"

Tom Howard put his finger on it: "Things have a way of falling to pieces. The shingles blow off the roof. The fender rusts through and the exhaust pipe drags. Cuffs fray, nylons run, hair falls out, joints stiffen, and wattles appear under our chins. Nothing is exempt, not even our ideas . . . .

"There was a noble law for human intercourse given at Sinai, and within a few hundred years it had deteriorated at the hands of its practitioners to a cynical array of functions. There was a new and energetic law announced in Judah, and within a few centuries it had calcified into a brittle and gorgeous object d'art . . . .

"We begin with something which we take to be pure and inviolable, and within a few years we find ourselves a thousand miles from where we began."[9]

That experience of growing out of a succession of safe chambers into ever larger ones is the story of the early days of my personal voyage of faith . . . perhaps yours as well.

My life began in the warm comfort and protection of a loving home. Although my mother and father were divorced shortly after I was born (if not because of it), love reigned in our home. We didn't have much else, really. But it didn't seem to matter. My mother worked long hours at whatever jobs she could find to provide for us during the final days of World War II. Yet she was always there at night to ask me about my day, to read to me from the Bible (especially the Psalms which we memorized together in the King James Version), to create fantastic bedtime tales of adventure, to tuck me in, and to *"lay me down to sleep," praying "the Lord my soul to keep."*

I came to believe that decency and order in my life were right up there with cleanliness and godliness (probably why I ended up a Presbyterian!). One of our family mottos was: "A place for everything . . . and everything in its place."

And I was meticulous—if not obsessive. There wasn't a thing out of place in my room. My clothes were always hung neatly, facing the same direction, color coded, and in order of descending size (which my wife will tell you is still true). My one pair of shoes was always shined. My school books were properly stacked every night, with the largest on the bottom and the smallest on the top. And it was important to me that my pencils were kept sharp and placed next to one another on my desk in a descending trajectory. Worst of all (or best, as I thought then), I would stack my coins in the same formation: half-dollars first since they were largest, then quarters, nickels, pennies, and dimes.

Everything in my life was properly ordered, even to the extent of my attending Military Academy in elementary school which I endured for the most part, with the possible exception of the mock battles which my schoolmates and I were required to perform on "Visitor Days." The one thing I most hated was shouldering that heavy rifle and shooting its blank bullets at my classmates on the "battlefield," who would then swoon dramatically and fall dead while our parents looked on with admiration and responded with voracious applause.

Still and all, it was a safe and ordered world in which I grew up, despite the international chaos surrounding us. As was the world of my childhood faith. My mother and grandmother practiced a loose combination of the teachings of Christian Science (my great grandmother was a Christian Science Practitioner), along with Religious Science, The Unity School of Christianity, and Norman Vincent Peale.

So I grew up knowing deep down:
- that God was Love . . .
- that nothing could separate me from that Love . . .
- that what seemed to be evil in the world was merely the misguided attempts of good people who had lost their way . . .
- that the Bible was the most beautiful book in the world (and the "Authorized" King James Version by far the best) . . .
- that Jesus was the ultimate expression of God's love, the greatest example of what humanity could become, and my personal friend . . .
- that one's purpose in life was to build the Kingdom of God on earth . . .

- that everyone regardless of race, creed, nationality, gender, color, sexual orientation, or economic status was a child of God . . .
- that Judaism and Christianity were complimentary religions (I had never heard of Islam) . . .
- that Jesus fully embodied the universal 'Christ Consciousness' and was a way-shower to others . . .
- that God, nature, the universe, and we human beings were all one . . .
- that since God is within all of us, "Greater things can you do" . . .
- that while we make our own choices in life, God coaxes us toward goodness and compassion, but does not punish nor sit in judgment . . . and
- that in the end, God can be trusted to protect us and bring us all home to live forever with Him/Her. (I never had a problem with inclusive language because we were taught that God is a Divine Spirit, not a human being, and we always spoke of, and prayed to, our "Father/Mother God.")

But the simple purity of my childhood faith, like shingles blown off the roof, was soon to degenerate into dogma.

I still am not sure what it was that drew me to what turned out to be a group of conservative evangelical students on my high school campus. I remember reading in our school newspaper that there was this group meeting after school in the cafeteria. "If you believe, come join us," the ad said. "If you don't, come and find out." So, since I thought I believed (whatever that meant), I went to the meeting . . . and ended up being befriended by a passionate group of born-again Christians earnestly attempting to "win our campus for Christ."

Perhaps it was their warm welcome of strangers that attracted me. Perhaps it was their certainty about the Bible, God, Jesus, salvation, and the afterlife. But most of all, it was the way they truly loved each other . . . and me.

I wrestled with their "dogmatic" beliefs for several years before consenting to go along with them. It was such an exclusivist set of convictions. Not only was the Bible inerrant and literally true ("God wrote it, I believed it, that settled it"), but human beings were *not* essentially good (as I had been taught). Rather, we were all sinners who needed to be saved, and Jesus had died to take our place on the cross so that we would not go to hell, but rather would be able to live forever in heaven with Jesus, God, and other born-again Christians (a notion which I now find to be at best boring, and at worst more like the other place!). All that I needed to do to was to pray a simple prayer: "Dear God, I believe that Jesus died to take away my sins. Please forgive me and come into my heart as my Savior and Lord." So I did.

That evangelical experience came to define my faith, or rather my beliefs, throughout college and for the few years following. We had such a simple clarity about everything in those days. There were no more questions to answer, no more problems with which to struggle. No more fuzziness of doubt. Only absolute certainty. And a passion for "souls" (not individuals!) which focused my energies toward one goal: sharing the Good News of Jesus with others. I felt embraced by like-minded believers, emboldened by the certainty and conviction of what we believed to be the truth, and passionate about being used by God to save my family and friends. Night after night I would pray to God for the salvation of my own mother (who year-after-year had taught me the Bible!), my grandmother, my brother, my stepfather, and my "unsaved" friends. I could not imagine them dying and spending a "Christless eternity in hell." It is this terrible religious conviction which ultimately and tragically divided our family for years.

All the while, my religious worldview was increasingly disconnected from what I was learning about the world—history, science, literature, language, psychology, sociology, world religions, and the like, but it didn't seem to matter that much. Somehow I learned to separate my religious life from the rest of my life. Like the pencils that needed to take their place in descending order and the coins that needed to stack up correctly, my beliefs needed to be dogmatically correct and Biblically defensible.

I can well relate to the experience of Fr. Tom Stella, a young Catholic priest in Berkeley, when he writes that "the religion of my youth was a great comfort on one hand, and a terrible burden on the other. There was a security in knowing what it took to be on the 'straight and narrow,' and in knowing that if I strayed, the way back was clearly marked—the well-trod path of repentance and confession. And there was comforting warmth that came from wrapping myself in the routine rituals that religion provided. They were like a cocoon, though I wonder now how much metamorphosis was taking place . . . . As with many others in my generation, the brand of religion I internalized was a matter of requirements that presumed God was *against* me rather than *for* me; it created a sense of self that hovered close to the minimum standard for acceptability."[10]

It was during that early phase of my spiritual quest that I chanced to read Tom Howard's delightful autobiography entitled, *Christ the Tiger*. (Actually, I think it was really about Tom the Tiger, but he was much too much the old-school Eastern Establishment type to say it!) I clearly understood what he meant when he wrote of his own back-to-the-womb experience:

"A baby is secure, warm and satisfied," he wrote. "If given his choice, he would stay there forever. He can neither imagine nor desire what is outside. If you told him how nice it is to have friends, and how good artichokes are, he would recoil in fear and disgust. The security that my religious friends enjoyed appeared to me in this light. Of course they were secure, I thought. They have opted out of most of what makes the world exciting and risky."[11]

I must tell you, I was deeply scarred during those years by religious fundamentalism. I still remember the terrible anger and devastation I later felt at being cheated out of so many experiences during the formative years of my life. But at least I survived my religion. A number of my close friends did not, and have ended up as bitter cynics. I am one of the lucky ones.

Over the past quarter-century I have come to thrive upon the daily adventure of a search for new truth, wherever it leads me. Through my personal readings, my post-graduate studies, travels, and conversations with people of many faiths (and none), from every conceivable ideology, nationality, and socio-economic background, I have come to understand that God is bigger than any of our ideas about God . . . that no one religion has absolute claim on the truth . . . that God's love and justice is for all people . . . and that it takes different forms in different cultures, times, and places.

As Dietrich Bonhoeffer asked, "Do we really believe that God loves us more than everyone else? How could we?"

While the Way of Jesus is still my path, my doorway, my approach into God's realm, I respect and encourage others to make their entrance into the same realm by their particular way, however different from my own. Human religions are like the windows in a grand cathedral in which each window is of a different motif. The radiance of the great light outside the cathedral creates any variety of beautiful colors and patterns in each of the windows, each different from the other. But the outside light, which illuminates each of the windows, is but One Light.

I believe that the Bible is a human book, not a divine book, that it is comprised of the stories of human beings down through the ages attempting to put words around their experiences of the Mystery of God, love, joy, and life . . .

- that the Bible seeks to open a conversation, not end one . . .
- that the Gospel is about living fully and humanly in this world, not just the next . . .
- that faith is about living by grace and love, not by fear and guilt . . .
- that true religion is about human fulfillment and social responsibility, not about meeting some religious or ethical requirements . . .
- that gender and sexual orientation, like color, age and nationality, are differences to be celebrated, not deviances to be corrected . . .

- that this kind of openness to life leads to liberation from self-preoccupation—personally, religiously, and politically . . .
- that this openness results in a life of joy, passion, compassion, inclusion, social betterment, and at times, confrontation with the powers that seek to silence it . . .
- that this world is the most important one because it is the only one we can work toward changing . . . and
- that true spiritual life is about being in relationship with a Sacred Reality here and now.

This is the joy and energizing passion of my life.

Each of our life stories is unique. Yet one of the common threads which weave us together is our continual need to be reborn and constantly open to the stirrings of new life within us. I know personally how traumatic it is to leave familiar beliefs, rituals, and camaraderie behind. The guilt and fear which one feels in even questioning the assumptions of one's own religious tradition are often excruciatingly painful. It can be very lonely to grow out-of-sync with a group of formerly like-minded people, to risk re-examining the formulas of faith and images of God, faith, church, nation, war, calling, and salvation with which one has been raised. But I also know what it feels like to be free, to be authentically myself. And I will never again go back into bondage.

Your life and faith experiences will be different from mine. But our common desire to discover a better way will keep us moving in the same direction. I trust that you will find it a mind-opening and heart-opening discovery as we begin to "Chart a New Course for Christianity."

So let us together come up on deck . . . stand together . . . breathe deeply . . . rock slowly with the pitch and roll of the ship . . . listen to the wind in the riggin' . . . get the drift of the sea . . . take a long look at the stars . . . .

And then chart our course for a New World.

CHAPTER 3

DRAGON TERRITORIES

"Following the light of the sun,
we left the Old World."

— CHRISTOPHER COLUMBUS

There is a curious thing about many of the maps of the ancient world. In the four corners the cartographer would inscribe a warning: *"THE WORLD ENDS HERE,"* or *"BE-YOND THIS POINT—THE DRAGONS."* Few sailors would risk even approaching that imaginary line of terror for fear of their lives.

Of course, as the science of navigation expanded, new captains took courage to go beyond the known world. Gradually those "dragon territories" diminished, as did the sailors' fears of piloting their ships in uncharted waters. Subsequent maps of the same territory would be labeled, *"MAPS OF THE ENTIRE WORLD."* And the edges of those maps would be inscribed with extensive notes on who first discovered what and when.

Good maps are our best effort at describing what we know. However, they are not the reality which they seek to describe. Some maps are better than other maps. As it was in ancient map-making, so it is today in science, sociology, medicine, art, business, philosophy, political science . . . in all of the liberal arts . . . especially in theology, religion, and ethics.

Why would those ancient maps appear so foreboding? Because of our terrible fear of the unknown. Fear has always been the primary factor inhibiting new knowledge and discovery. While fear can sometimes serve a positive end in suggesting appropriate caution, fear has also served countless negative ends in curtailing curiosity, imagination, creativity, and new discovery. Fear keeps us frozen in our certainties, rigid in our positions, and inflexible in our religious compassions.

Yet, "the only thing we have to fear is fear itself."

Recently, journalists Bill and Judith Moyers were awarded the Union Seminary of New York's highest honor, the Union Medal. In a moving and prophetic address, Bill put his finger on the pulse of the problem and issued a challenge to the next generation:

"The spirit of truth is under assault . . . . Stand for truth.
Democracy is in peril . . . . Stand for democracy.
Religion has bowed again to power and privilege . . . .

Stand for justice—and the faith that liberates
  God from partisan agendas.
America is not the country it can be. We're troubled by fear . . . .
Remind us of America's promise—and stand for the courage
  to fulfill it."

Moyers concluded his stirring address by declaring, "Christian Realism . . . requires us to see the world as it is, without illusions, and then take it on. With love, of course. But a certain kind of love . . . . Reinhold Niebuhr put it this way: 'When we talk about love we have to become mature or we will become sentimental. Basically love means . . . being responsible . . . toward our family, toward our civilization, and now by pressures of history, toward the universe of humankind.'"[12]

As I write this chapter, I am working with a buddy of mine restoring a small 25-year-old cruising boat. I have been learning how to set what they called "Waypoints" on the boat's GPS (Global Positioning System). A Waypoint is a navigational marker one sets at a certain latitude and longitude to fix a point of reference for future excursions. A sequence of Waypoints marks a safe path from which you can confidently set a new course the next time. A Waypoint provides one with a safe haven from which to launch a new journey of discovery.

My plan in this book is to bring into play a number of current developments in theology, Biblical studies, world religions, sociology, and ethics and to suggest where I see progressive Christianity positioned on the bigger map of what God is doing in the world today. From this I will suggest a number of new "Waypoints" from which we can navigate our future voyages.

One way to look at Christianity is as a "map of the soul." From its inception, Christian faith has been described as a "way" or a "journey" or a "path," rather than an intellectual assent to a number of propositional statements of correct belief, or a set of religious rules. This is how Christianity began—not as a religion, or a code of law, but as a Way of Life. The community which wrote

John's Gospel has Jesus saying, "I am the Way." The early followers of Jesus were called, "Followers of The Way," not "Believers in
the Doctrine." Before Emperor Constantine, Christianity was defined by its *actions*, not by its *beliefs*. The very term "Christian"
meant "Little Christ," not a religious institution.

Here is my premise: The old maps of Christian belief, ethics,
and the Bible, built upon even more ancient creedal systems,
served an important role in the development of human knowledge, culture, and faith. But many of those ancient maps are woefully out of date—not merely woefully, but dangerously out of sync
with the world as we know it today and with God as we experience
God in our world. We see the result of this disconnect in the expo-
nential rise of religious orthodoxies, terror, and fundamentalism.

However, the past is but a prologue to the future. I hope that
this experience will be for each of us a new way of seeing, a new
way of believing, a new way of trusting, and a new way of making
a difference in the world—a desperately needed change of course
in an increasingly violent, disillusioned, dangerous, and uncaring
world. "To see the world as it is, without illusions," as Moyers put
it, "and then take it on."

There are certain individuals, churches, and groups around the
country who are working intentionally to set a new course for
Christianity. The church I serve is one of them. We are a community of Christians and those of other faiths (or none) who are discovering a fresh approach to God through the life and teachings of
Jesus and our life together. Part of this journey is about celebrating
the faithfulness and camaraderie of those who have other names
for their ways into God's realm. In fact, we are a "spiritual home"
for a number of folks of other faiths (and none), and understand
the sharing of bread and wine in Jesus' name to be a representation
of an ancient vision of God's feast for all people.[13]

As progressive Christians, we believe that God still speaks to us
not only through the Biblical stories and creeds, but through all of
life, especially through one another. We are continually discovering new ways to reconnect our spirits without disconnecting our

minds. We are intentionally seeking to be an inclusive community of love and justice.

Speaking at his Installation Service as the new Dean of the Washington National Cathedral in 2005, The Very Rev. Samuel T. Lloyd said the following:

> *"I believe this cathedral is called to be a major voice of a faith that is firm at the center and soft at the edges . . . a faith that embraces ambiguity and that honors other faiths . . . a faith that insists that Christ's values be embodied in the social order."*

That is precisely what I believe each of our churches and religious communities is called to be for this new century.

Leadership for this new movement must come from the laity as well as the clergy—from the pew not just the pulpit. As the Norwegian playwright, Henrik Ibsen, put it: *"A community is like a ship; everyone ought to be prepared to take the helm."* And, I would add, with the tremendous challenge ahead of us all, we need all hands on deck!

In Jewish folk art, the "new creation" is often pictured as an ark riding safely upon a restless sea. In early Christian art, the church was often depicted as a ship under sail, traversing troubled waters. We might consider this prayer an "Act of Commissioning" for our Grand Voyage together in charting a new course for Christianity:

> *"Eternal Father, strong to save,*
> *Whose arm doth bid the restless wave,*
> *Who biddest the mighty ocean deep*
> *Its own appointed limits keep:*
> *O hear us when we cry to thee*
> *For those in peril on the sea . . .*
>
> *O Trinity of love and power,*
> *Our brethren shield in danger's hour;*
> *From rock and tempest, fire and foe,*

Protect them whereso'er they go:
And ever let there rise to Thee
Glad hymns of praise from air and land and sea."[14]

CHAPTER 4

THE ABSENCE OF GOD

Men go abroad to wonder
at the height of mountains,
at the huge waves of the sea,
the long courses of the rivers,
at the vast compass of the ocean,
at the circulating motions of the stars,
and they pass by themselves without wondering.
—SAINT AUGUSTINE

A recent international Associated Press poll asked the question: "Which of the following comes closest to expressing what you feel about God?" Americans responded this way:

1%   I am not sure.

2%   I don't believe in God.

2%   I find myself believing in God some of the time not at others.

4%   I don't know whether there is a God, and I don't believe there is a way to find out.

10%   While I have doubts, I feel that I do believe in God.

11%   I don't believe in a personal God, but I do believe in a higher power of some kind.

70%   I know God really exists, and I have no doubts about it.[15]

This is amazing to me! Because if there's one thing I've learned about social correctness over the years, it is this: If you want to stop other people from having a really good time at a party, start talking about God! Really! There is nothing quite like it. It is amazing how many intelligent people say they believe in God but would never think of talking about it!

I love what William Sloane Coffin said about being at a faculty gathering of good friends at Yale when he was the University Chaplain, and saying to a colleague, "Isn't the existence of God a lively question?"

To which the political scientist colleague answered, "Bill, it's not even a question, let alone a lively one!"[16]

But I'm with Bill. Some of the most engaging conversations I have been part of have been around the great mysteries of life.

More often than not, when someone talks to me about God, it is not to tell me why they do, but why they do not believe in God. When I ask them to tell me about the God they don't believe in, it usually turns out to be a God I don't believe in either—often a personification of a bad experience they had with a certain type of religion or with religious people:

- A father who beat them into compliance . . .
- A mother who insulated them from the real world . . .
- A sense of adolescent shame . . .
- An inability to accept one's sexuality . . .
- A spouse who used religion as a weapon . . .
- A preacher who harangued them with guilt . . .
- A simplistic world view that no longer works for them . . .
- An uncritical view of the Bible . . .
- An unrealistic view of the Church . . .
- A mishmash of God, America, and Apple Pie . . .
- A fairytale God who promised to give them their every wish . . .
- A justification for war or inhumane treatment of others . . .
- A blind faith in America as God's chosen nation.

One thing I have found to be true in my experience is that you can't outgrow God. God has been around for a lot longer than you and I, and will doubtless continue to be around long after we have gone. What we can outgrow are our limited concepts of God. And that's not only OK, it's a good thing—because we are always growing and changing. And God is big enough to stay ahead of our learning curve.

So how can we know, or say, anything about God?

In her comprehensive book, *A History of God*, Karen Armstrong points out that even in what we have called "The Abrahamic Tradition" (that is to say, the common source of three of the world's great religions: Judaism, Christianity, and Islam), there never was a common, objective view of God. Each generation of the Abrahamic religions developed its own religious traditions to create the image of God that worked for it. That included various names, identities, actions, and requirements by the deity. She writes:

"The idea of God formed in one generation by one set of human beings could be meaningless in another. "Indeed, the statement 'I believe in God' has no objective meaning, as such, but like any other statement only means something in context, when proclaimed by a particular community. Consequently there is no one, unchanging idea contained in the word 'God.' Instead, the word contains a whole spectrum of meanings, some of which are contradictory or even mutually exclusive."[17]

The best hint we have at a self-definition of God in the Bible is from the Book of Exodus. Perhaps you remember the story. Moses had heard God tell him to take off on a dangerous Freedom March and lead a motley disorganized tribe of thousands of Israelites (former Palestinians) out from under the oppression of their government in Egypt to freedom in a promised land they would call the new Canaan.

Of course Moses balks at the offer, knowing that he and his followers might well be killed escaping from the mighty Egyptian army. So he demands of God (who happens to be speaking to him from the flames of a burning bush, of all places!) an answer to two questions:

- First, "Who am I to say this?" to which God answers: "Don't worry, it's not about you! I will be with you." (Thank you very much!)
- And second, "When King Pharaoh asks me who it is that sent me to him, what should I say?" To which God replies, "Tell him, 'I Am Who I Am,' and I have sent you." (Hello?)

"I AM WHO I AM." That is the clearest statement we have from God. While that may play well in armchair philosophical discussions with a meerschaum and a wee dram of single-malt, it is not a crowd-stopper at cocktail parties!

"Tell him, 'I Am Who I Am!'"

There you have it! It must have worked for Moses, but let me tell you, it's never worked very well for me!

Maybe the reason that it did work for Moses was that it was a way of speaking of God without "naming" God. To name someone, or something, in the ancient world (and even today) was a way of defining it, controlling it, reducing it, becoming its master.

Toward the end of Moses' life, it was said that even though he had a number of "conversations" with this "I Am Who I Am," Moses was not satisfied. He felt that he did not have the authority to speak to the people about "I Am" because he had never seen Him (or It). (A healthy reticence I could wish for many convinced Christians today!) Yahweh initially refuses, but reluctantly agrees to give Moses a look-see. But Moses must crouch down behind a rock and peek through a crack in the rock as God passes by. Even at that, God tells Moses that he will only see his backside. A more common translation is, "You shall see only my tail."

The point of the story is that Isaiah was right. In Isaiah 45:15, one of the greatest prophets of all time declares, "God is the hidden God." The best we can hope to see are occasional faint "glimpses" or "intimations" of God. And even then, what we see is not so much God as "the footprints of God," the faint outline left by the vanished Mystery. "No one has seen God," the Bible says. Like the empty tomb, all that's left is grave clothes, radiant light, and imagination.

Novelist Frederick Buechner once fantasized that we all walk out some October evening and see, emblazoned across the evening sky in neon, the words, "I EXIST." Wouldn't that be terrific? All our doubts would disappear. Of course, he was referring to God. But these days it would be just as likely to read into that night sky, "ME! ME! ME!"

Moses wanted to have it all, but in the end, all that he was allowed was a glance at God's "backside." Isn't that the case with us? Time and again, we want a visual sighting. We want to see the majesty of God's glory and power right here, right now. And the best that we get is a lightning flash of mystery, disappearing as quickly as it appeared.

The great neo-orthodox German theologian, Karl Barth, having written a dozen thick volumes describing in loving, dogmatic detail the nature of God in Christ, comes to the conclusion: "In faith itself we are forced to say that our knowledge of God begins in all seriousness with the knowledge of the hiddenness of God...."[18]

"The day when God is absent, when He is silent," says Anthony Bloom, "is the beginning of prayer."[19]

Moses wanted a glimpse of God's *glory*. God says, "I'll show you my *goodness*." We want to see God's *power*. What we are given is God's *promise*.

Actually, the Hebrew is better translated, not "My presence will go with you," but, "My presence will go . . . ." God has not promised to "move in" with us, to be tamed and domesticated by us and limited to us. God has promised to go . . . to go on ahead of us...to pave the way for us through the wilderness, into the promised land.

This living, moving God is large, vital, free, and life-giving. You cannot see this God face-to-face and live. What you can see is the goodness of God, the acts of love and mercy toward a sometimes wayward, but still divinely beloved, people.

The questions for each of us are not, "What about *me*?" "Will God go with *me*?" The only important question is, "Will *I* go with this God?" Risking everything, trusting the invisible, stepping out on faith, not sight, following after the backside of God . . . will we go with this God?

Paul Tillich, arguably one of America's most important theologians, realized how difficult it is to talk about God. He even suggested that we stop using the word "God" for at least a hundred years so that we can purge the word of all of its meaningless and confusing baggage.

The clearest way for me to think about God is to look at how Jesus experienced God. Jesus had little to say *descriptively* about God, but a lot to show for how he *experienced* God. His experience was direct, transformative, and personal. God was to him "Abba," father and mother. And "Ruach," spirit, wind, and breath.

Like the ever-present invisible wind on the open sea, God is always present within, around, and through all of life. We can't see it directly. We can only experience it and see its results. God is the energy all around us—the source of all life and love, of all justice, resolve, passion, and compassion, of all truth and beauty, goodness and hope, wholeness and restoration.

In fact, those themes play very well at a cocktail party. And it is not much of a stretch to say that God is expressed in those ideals, wherever they are found. God is experienced in those actions. That is the big difference between God and Religion.

"Religion is primarily a search for security and not a search for truth. Religion is what we so often use to bank the fires of our anxiety. That is why religion tends toward becoming excessive, neurotic, controlling and even evil. That is why a religious government is always a cruel government."[20]

As a progressive Christian, I (and, I would bet, many of you) find more grace in the search for meaning than in dogmatic certainty—more value in questioning than in absolutes—and more energy in living life passionately than in denying it, or protecting myself from it.

With Bill Coffin, "I believe the power of God is lodged in the very marrow of our substance and is pressing, constantly pressing, for release in order to permeate every fiber of our being. And the demand is not for self-denial, as is so often preached, but rather for self-discovery and self-fulfillment of human life. This I think is what St. Paul means when he says, 'God searches our inmost being' and 'The kingdom of God consists not in words but in power.' To think we can escape wrestling with this power is to dream."[21]

So, please, tell me about the God you don't believe in. And I will tell you about the God in whom I deeply believe, but about whom I often have my doubts! Because for me, the most important question is not, "Do I believe in God?" but rather, "Does God believe in me?" and always, the answer is "YES."

"Faith is being grasped by the power of love, and there are many atheists with 'believing hearts.'"[22]

CHAPTER 5

ENTERING THE DEEP SEA OF MYSTERY

In your hands we rest,
in the cup of whose hands
an ark sailed rudderless
and without mast.

In your hands we rest,
and own a providence
as large as sea and sky
that could make
of the aimless wandering of the ark
a new beginning for the world.

In your hands we rest,
ready and content this day.

We are the boat.
We are the sea.
I sail in you.
You sail in me.

DAILY PRAYER OF DR. ALAN JONES,
DEAN OF GRACE CATHEDRAL, SAN FRANCISCO

"What is called knowledge in everyday parlance is only a small island in a vast sea that has not been traveled . . . ," writes Catholic theologian Karl Rahner. "Hence the existential question for the knower is this: Which does he love more, the small island of his so-called knowledge or the sea of infinite mystery?"

It is far easier and certainly more comfortable to stay on one's small island of knowledge and be an expert in a familiar mind-set than it is to venture out into the unknown. As Professor Huston Smith put it: "The larger the island of knowledge, the longer the shoreline of wonder."

In ancient times, our forbearers were overwhelmed with the wonder, awe, and mystery in all of nature. Every bush, every tree, every rock was sacred. To accidentally touch a sacred tree or step on a sacred stone was to disturb the eternal order of things and incur the wrath of the gods who indwelt them. There was in those early days no separation of physical from spiritual, sacred from secular, nature from God. Every day the world began again, fresh from the hands of God.

In his classic book, *Zorba the Greek*, Nikos Kazantzakis captures this primitive sense of life emerging fresh from the womb. Speaking of Zorba, the Boss says:

"Things we are accustomed to, and which we pass by indifferently, suddenly rise up in front of Zorba like fearful enigmas. Seeing a woman pass by, he stops in consternation.

"'What is that mystery?' he asks. 'What is a woman, and why does she turn our heads? Just tell me, I ask you, what's the meaning of that?'

"He interrogates himself with the same amazement when he sees a man, a tree in blossom, a glass of cold water. Zorba sees everything every day as if for the first time.

"We were sitting yesterday in front of the hut. When he had drunk a glass of wine, he turned to me in alarm:

"'Now, whatever is this red water, boss, just tell me! An old stock grows branches, and at first there's nothing but a sour bunch of beads hanging down. Time passes, the sun ripens them, they become as sweet as honey, and then they're called grapes. We trample on them; we extract the juice and put it into casks; it ferments on its own, we open it on the feast day of St. John the Drinker, it's become wine! It's a miracle! You drink the red juice and, lo and behold, your soul grows big, too big for the old carcass, it challenges God to a fight. Now tell me, boss, how does it happen?'

"I did not answer. I felt, as I listened to Zorba, that the world was recovering its pristine freshness. All the dulled daily things regained the brightness they had in the beginning, when we came out of the hands of God. Water, women, the stars, bread, returned to their mysterious, primitive origin and the diving whirlwind burst once more upon the air.'"[23]

One of my favorite books in my student years was J.B. Phillips', *Your God Is Too Small*. In the 1960's, Phillips was seeking to address this widening gap between our "Sunday School theology" and the broadening vistas of science. He wrote, "Many men and women today are living without any faith in God . . . not because they are wicked or selfish . . . but because they have not found in their adult minds a God big enough to account for life, big enough to fit in with the new scientific age, big enough to command their highest admiration and respect."

So let's take a little "rational trouble over mystery," as Barth called it. Take, for instance, the name we give to Mystery: "G-O-D." Most of us have spoken that Name, used it in a conversation, perhaps even conversed with it, or heard it speaking to us. Many people use it when referring to great pain, or great pleasure. Many nations ask that Name to bless them, as well as to curse their enemies—as do football teams.

Others call the Mystery by other names: "Great Spirit" to Native Americans; "Allah" to Muslims; "JHWH" or "Jehovah" or "The Holy One" to Jews; "Father" to Christians; "Mother" to Wiccas; "Nature" to pantheists; "The Force" to Star Wars fans; etc.

Of course, we have given God a name because of our need to speak intelligently about an unintelligible experience, both personal and cosmic. But it is that very anthropomorphic image that limits our understanding of God. The God of my experience may well not be anything like the God of your experience. Even Jesus' understanding of God came out of his direct personal experience. Jesus called God by the intimate endearment of a child, "Abba," "Father." And God is said to have announced to Jesus, "Thou art my beloved Son."

But the word Jesus uses most often of God is the Hebrew word, "Ruach," which translates, "wind" and "breath," as well as "spirit." We cannot see the wind; we can only experience its effects. Breath is a wind inside our body. God is that which breathes into us life, that which energizes us from within. Whatever that force or energy is that breathes life into what would otherwise have been lifeless, inert, and inorganic is God. Jesus experienced this energy as presence, love, affirmation, rebuke, empowerment, justice, courage, passion, and compassion.

Perhaps "mysteries" must forever remain so. To define them risks losing their power over/under/within us. Rather than attempting to figure out the Mystery of God, I invite you to enter into it.

"Suppose," says Jack Spong, "that God is defined [not as a 'heavenly parent' who acts to relieve us of personal responsibility], but as the *Source of Life*, so that our worship demands that we cooperate with all of nature rather than trying to conquer it for our own benefit . . . .

"Suppose God is defined as the *Source of Love*, so that our worship enables us to journey beyond the limits of our fear to embrace all that is . . . .

"Suppose God is defined as the *Ground of Being* so that our worship relates us to a holiness that permeates all that is.

"That is what we need to understand before we human beings can grow up and accept responsibility for our world."[24]

"We are the boat, we are the sea,
I sail in you, you sail in me."

CHAPTER 6

FATHER GOD OR MOTHER NATURE?

I arise today, through the strength of Heaven:

Light of Sun,

Brilliance of Moon,

Splendour of Fire,

Speed of Lightning,

Swiftness of Wind,

Depth of Sea,

Stability of Earth,

Firmness of Rock . . .

(THE BREASTPLATE OF ST. PATRICK)

"The man whispered, 'God, speak to me.'
And a meadowlark sang. But the man did not hear.

'So the man yelled, 'God, speak to me!'
Thunder rolled across the sky. But the man did not listen.

"The man looked around and said, 'God, let me see you.'
And the stars shined brightly. But the man did not notice.

"And the man shouted, 'God, show me a miracle.'
And a life was born. But the man did not know.

"So, the man cried out in despair,
'Touch me God, and let me know you are here.'

"Whereupon, God reached down and touched the man.
But the man brushed the butterfly away and walked on."

In the beginning, God was everywhere. There was nowhere that God was not. God was in the fire, the earth, the air, and water. As the exiled Lords in the lush Forest of Arden in Shakespeare's, "As You Like It," declared, there were:

"...tongues in trees, books in the running brooks,
sermons in stones, and good in everything."[25]

But it was not long before this common belief in the divinity of nature was squelched by materialism and "scientific" thinking. God was removed from creation, the spirit dissected from matter, leaving only the "disenchantment of nature." With the exception of the artists, poets, and philosophers, this thing called "anima," "the breath of life," "the soul," "God," was banished to one of two places: the human heart, or heaven. Either you were a "theist" and believed in a transcendent God who, like a divine clockmaker, wound up the world and refused to intervene as it wound down, or you were a "pantheist" who believed that "everything is God."

Those were my choices in the conservative churches of my youth. I could either be a "theist" and believe that God was a kind of benign landlord, or I could be a "pantheist" and believe that God and nature were the same thing.

Since I could not buy the idea that the snails that I accidentally stepped on were as divine as my girlfriend (most of the time), I couldn't be a pantheist. So I became a theist. Better said, I became a Christian theist. I believed in a God who at some point in the distant past created the world, and that people like myself ended up ruining it—so much so that God had to send God's self into that world, in the form of a human being, to save us from that world.

I remember the very street corner in Pacific Palisades, California, where my Rabbi friend and I were standing during the social unrest of the late 1960's. He said to me, "Gary, it's well and good that you have a passion for saving souls. But what about a passion for saving not just their souls but saving their entire beings? These people are God's greatest acts of creation and yet they are dying daily of loneliness, prejudice, hatred, greed, selfishness, meaninglessness, boredom, and apathy. And further, what about our society which is dying of injustice, countries which are dying of war, and the earth which is dying of plunder? Doesn't your God care about any of that?"

That, as they say, was my "wake up call"!

My Jewish colleague was right. In my small theological box, this wonderful world that the Bible proclaimed God had created so very good, seemed to be of little value in the bigger picture of things. The earth was so transient, we were taught, it wasn't worth saving. So in our church we didn't talk much about what we might do to improve the world. We did not talk about how we might empower people who were suffering and dying in it. Nor did we do anything to try to save nature from exploitation or nuclear extinction. After all, we were told, we are only here for a short time and the world was going to hell in a handbasket, so why should we waste time trying to fix it? Social betterment was a waste of time, much like rearranging deck chairs on the Titanic. We should be about the task of preaching the Gospel and living a spiritual life (whatever that meant).

That was the beginning of my conversion to what one of my seminary professors called "this worldliness" of the Gospel. Over the years, those two ways of thinking about God and the world (either theism or pantheism) have worn pretty thin for me. I came to a place some time ago where I needed a bigger God. And I needed to see myself as a participant with God in the process of saving the world. As our Jewish friends put it, to become part of the great commission of "tikun-olam," "repairing the world."

I found that I had many more questions than answers about God, life, ethics, prayer, humanness, and salvation. And I realized that the confines of Christian orthodoxy were no longer satisfying to me—intellectually, emotionally, or pragmatically. But I could not keep from feeling guilty about it.

With Tom Stella, "I have come to realize that most guilt is the result of growth. Imagine yourself as a small child standing inside a box. As long as you do not touch the box—the walls of restriction placed around you by parents, religious authority, and the conventional attitudes of the culture—you feel comfortable, content, and guiltless. But as you grow, you become too big for the space. Guilt is what is felt when your body touches the walls of your box. Even *thinking* 'outside the box' can feel wrong, but the real wrong, the ultimate tragedy, would be to live small, to fit into rather than outgrow your confines, to recoil with each pang of conscience . . . . When we confront life's inconsistencies with religion's explanations, life [always] wins . . . . If we are to remain people of faith, and if God is to continue to have relevance in our lives, we must think and believe in ways other than we have."[26]

For me, this process began by re-thinking what I believed about God. In the first place, although I often would use the language, I did not believe in a literal "Father God." God is not a Divine Parent who requires our perfection, demands our discipline, or coddles our childishness. God is not a human being. God is a Sacred Spirit, beyond gender and stereotype. That is why there are frequently times in our church when we speak of God as "She," or "Mother/Father God," or "Divine Spirit," or "the Eternal." When we say that, we mean much more than "divine parent." We mean "our source of all life and love."

Having said that, I do not believe in a "Mother Nature." Yes, nature is alive and pulsating with the creative impulse of God. "Earth's crammed with heaven, and every common bush afire with God," as Elizabeth Barrett Browning put it. But nature is not God. Nature is capricious. Nature is capable of great devastation as well as wonder and great beauty. Nature and God are interrelated. God is in nature; but God is not defined by nature. God speaks to us in every molecule of nature, but we have grown deaf to hearing God's voice. That's why we began our annual "Blessing of the Animals Service" some years ago (during which we lay hands on horses, llamas, goats, pigs, snakes, and caterpillars in the sanctuary because we share with them a common creaturehood.) We preach about the earth and the environment in our worship services and are seeking ways to preserve and protect it for our posterity.

There are fundamental differences between God and the world: "God is necessary, the world is contingent; God is eternal, the world is limited in duration; God is infinite, the world is finite; God is by nature morally perfect, and the world—well, that one is obvious."[27]

But if one does not believe in a "Father God" (theism), or in a "Mother Nature" (pantheism), then what can we believe in? What I have found helpful is the idea of "pan-en-theism," a word that suggests not that everything is God, but that God is in everything —"all-in-God." God is interdependent with the world. God is more than the universe, yet the universe is in God. God is not "somewhere else," God is "right here." God is not so much a Supernatural Being "out there" as a Sacred Mystery at the center of existence, the encompassing spirit in whom everything that is, is. God is all around us and within us. God infuses and enfolds all living things. "In God we live and move and have our being."[28]

As Martin Luther said of the sacraments, so we say of the universe. God is "in, with, and under," not just the bread and wine, but all life—animate and inanimate.

Panentheism is not a modern invention. It is actually the earliest concept of God. God is at one and the same time, transcendent (meaning God is outside of creation), and immanent (meaning God is present within creation), and encompasses all life in a unity of love.

When the apostle Paul addressed those philosophers atop Mars Hill in Athens, next to the Acropolis, he began by commending them, saying, "Athenians, I see how extremely religious you are in every way. For as I went through the city and looked carefully at the objects of your worship, I found among them an altar with the inscription, 'To an Unknown God.' What therefore you worship as unknown, this I proclaim to you . . . . For 'in him we live and move and have our being' as even some of your own poets have said, 'For we too are his offspring.'"[29]

I wonder if fundamentalist Christianity today—with its worship of the Bible, its dogmatic adherence to select sentences of scripture, its religious intolerance, its right-wing fanaticism, and its American God—has not become like the Greek's religion of old, encased in philosophies and 'shrines made of human hands,' picturing God as 'like gold, or silver, or stone, an image formed by the art and imagination of mortals,' as if they were God.

In the history of philosophy, there have been several distinct ways of thinking about God and God's relationship with the world:

Atheism initially referred to anyone who expressed disbelief in the State gods. Socrates, for example, was a very religious man but was charged with disseminating atheism in speaking against the Divine Caesars. In Christian usage, the term came to be applied to anyone who in any way questions the existence of God.

Close to it is Agnosticism, which is often used to describe those who cannot find sufficient evidence to believe in God, and therefore are content not to know.

Deism is an 18th century concept of a religion based on reason alone. It assumes a mechanistic view of the universe in which God created the world but thereafter refused to intervene in its operation. The universe is a machine, like a clock, created perfectly by a divine clockmaker, and left to wind down of its own accord.

Polytheism denotes the existence of any number of transcendent and personal gods.

Pantheism means literally "everything God." "God is everything and everything is God." It is used of those systems in which God and Nature (or God and the universe) are synonymous.

I believe each of these ideas to be inadequate explanations of God. In the history of Christianity, there are two remaining philosophies. These could be called "supernatural theism" and "panentheism":

Supernatural theism, the time-honored way of thinking about God, imagines God as a person-like being. God created the world sometime ago and is entirely separate from it. God is "up in heaven," "out there," "beyond the universe." As Marcus Borg puts it, with supernatural theism, the God-world relationship is seen in interventionist terms. Throughout history God has allowed the world to run its own course, with occasional spectacular interventions from God from the outside. These would include any number of unexplained phenomena in the Bible, like Joshua making the sun stand still, like God speaking to Moses from a burning bush or to the prophet Balaam through the prophet's donkey, and like the water of the Red Sea stacking on top of itself to allow thousands of Israelites to walk across on dry land, while demolishing thousands of Egyptians. In the Apocrypha and the New Testament these divine interventions are most often clustered around Jesus: his birth, miracles, death, and resurrection.

Panentheism, a more recent way of thinking about God, imagines God and the God-world relationship differently. Although the word, "panentheism," is only about two hundred years old, the notion is very ancient. Rather than imagining God as a person-like being "out there," this concept imagines God as the encompassing

Spirit in whom everything that is, is. The universe is not separate from God, but is in God . . . *pan* means "everything," *en* means "in," and *theism* comes from the Greek word for God, "Theos."

Panentheism is not to be confused with pantheism. Pantheism says that everything that is (pan) is God (theism). But clearly not everything that is, is God. While I have great respect for all of life, I do not worship the trees and the animals, nor do I recoil in terror before an angry nature deity who lashes out in fury through earthquakes, tsunami disasters, hurricanes, and cracked levees.

So when I say that I am a panentheist, what I mean is that I believe that everything is in God, and that God is in everything. That is what Paul was referring to in the Book of Acts when he told those Athenian philosophers, "just as some of your poets have said, God is the One in whom we live and move and have our being." God is not "out there," apart from us; God is "in here," one with us. "Rather than speaking of '*divine intervention*,' panentheism speaks of '*divine intention*,' and '*divine interaction*.' Or, to use sacramental language, it sees the presence of God 'in, with, and under' everything—not as the direct cause of events, but as presence beneath and within our everyday lives."[30]

In my own journey of faith, I have come to the place where supernatural theism no longer fits with my experience of God. I find that panentheism does. Panentheism factors in both God's immanence and God's transcendence. God is, and always has been, with me and within me. And I am, and have always been, within God. Further, God is with and within the entire cosmos, and all life that has ever been present on the earth is within God.

As John Zuck says, "No view of God is larger than the Panentheistic view. All other theisms (deism, theism, polytheism, animism, pantheism, atheism) are fragmented theologies compared to panentheism. This is the ground for an inexhaustible faith—that God is present right now, in every cell of our bodies, in every beat of our hearts, in every person, in every star, in every loving thought, birthing every particle of every atom of the entire Creation into a constant stream of existence, the invisible Nothing and Nowhere that brings forth Everything and Everywhere. God in all things and all things in God invites wonder, and wonder invites all to touch God."[31]

Philip Clayton describes this as "emergence." "Traditional theology looked backward: It postulated God as the cause of all things. Emergent theology looks forward: It postulates God as the goal toward which all things are heading . . . . In this model God sets in motion a process of ongoing creativity . . . . God is no longer the cosmic lawgiver. The result is a far cry from Calvin's God, who must predestine all outcomes 'before the foundation of the world.' Instead, God guides the process of creativity. God, nature and creatures together compose the melodies of the unfolding world, as it were, without preordaining the outcome . . . . In Philip Hefner's beautiful phrase, we become 'created co-creators' with God."[32]

I have always experienced a personal relationship with God, and that most clearly through Jesus Christ. With Marcus Borg, "I am persuaded that God has more the quality of a "presence" than of a nonpersonal "energy" or "force." To use Rabbi Martin Buber's language, I am persuaded that God has more the quality of a "you" than of an "it," more the quality of a "person" than that of an impersonal "source." I understand this sense of God as a presence, as a "you," not an "it." I also see it reflected in the centrality of the notion of covenant in the Jewish and Christian traditions. The Ever-Creating God made a divine covenant with the earth, then with Abraham and his descendents, then with all people.

Moreover, I think God "speaks" to us. I do not mean divine dictation. But I think God "speaks" to us—sometimes dramatically in visions, and sometimes more subtly in our dreams, in internal "proddings" or "leadings," through other people, through the events of our lives, through the devotional practices and scriptures of our tradition, and through all of creation.

That's what Presbyterian author Frederick Buechner means when he writes, "Listen to your life. Listen to what happens to you because it is through what happens to you that God speaks . . . .

It's in language that's not always easy to decipher, but it's there: powerfully, memorably, unforgettably."

God is always creating, always birthing new life: in the seed that transforms into a blade of grass, in the caterpillar cocoon which transforms into a butterfly, in the delicate plant which bravely thrusts it way through the hardened earth, in the sunflower whose head follows the sun throughout the day, from East to West, and in the human heart that "pants for God like a deer pants for the water brook." God is alive in the world.

God, for me, is the source of life, the source of love, the Ground of all Being. I agree with Jack Spong when he says that God is life, and we worship God by *living fully*. God is love, and we worship God by *loving wastefully*. God is Being, and we worship God by having the courage *to be all that we can be*. Ultimately, it is in the act of living, loving, and being that we go beyond the boundaries of our existence and experience the reality of transcendence, otherness, and eternity. God is not dead. God has entered into us, and we have entered into God. We are God-bearers, co-creators, incarnations of what God is in the world.

As one of our newly-confirmed young adults described it (having just returned from a spiritual pilgrimage to the island of Iona, Scotland): "Life is a journey with many paths, leading in many different directions. Parents and friends can only guide you part of the way. God is a powerful guide inside all of us. [God] is the presence that lets us know the right path."

Or, as another confirmand put it, "When there is light, we can see. And upon seeing, we can know where we are, who we are with, and what is available for us to do. Light inside of us allows us to see who we are and how we can develop into what we want to become. I believe that God is this light inside us."

And another proclaimed, "God is our savior, our strength, our mother, our father, and gives us love to nurture and unite us."

The life of faith is never boring, regardless of our age. There is always an opportunity to grow and stretch waiting for us around the next corner.

What would it mean for us to live every moment as though God were creating the world for the very first time through us? The dynamic life-force we call God is moving within and between us even as we connect ourselves through the pages of this book, breaking open the hardened crusts of our lives, and seeking cracks in our conformity through which we can create the world anew.

We have a choice: we can open ourselves to the power of that new life surging within us, or we can "brush the butterfly away and walk on."

But if we do, we will never again be able to sing,

> *Morning has broken like the first morning,*
> *Blackbird has spoken like the first bird . . .*
> *Sweet the rain's new fall sunlit from heaven,*
> *Like the first dewfall on the first grass . . .*
> *Mine is the sunlight! Mine is the morning*
> *Born of the one light Eden saw play!*
> *Praise with elation, praise every morning,*
> *God's re-creation of the new day!* [33]

CHAPTER 7

DEAD IN THE WATER

*"I believe that at the core of the universe is a
divine heartbeat of love, incredible and inaudible.
The purpose of our lives is to get close
enough to that heartbeat so that it
beats through us—so that that love becomes
audible and credible through our lives."*
—THE REV. DR. ALAN MAKER,
FORMER MODERATOR, GENERAL ASSEMBLY,
PRESBYTERIAN CHURCH OF SOUTHERN AFRICA

I am told that the Amazon River is the largest river in the world. The mouth is 90 miles across. There is enough water surging within it to exceed the flow of the Yangtze, Mississippi, and Nile Rivers combined. So much water comes from the Amazon that they can detect its currents 200 miles out into the Atlantic Ocean.

Yet one of the ironies of ancient navigation is that hundreds of sailors died in those very places for lack of water. They were at the mouth of the river, but they were dying of thirst. Sometimes captains of other ships from South America who knew the area would come alongside and call out, "What is your problem?" And they would exclaim, "Can you spare us some water? Our sailors are dying of thirst!" Then from the other ship would come the cry, "Just lower your buckets. You are in the mouth of the mighty Amazon River!"

This, I suggest, is the sad desperation of 21st century Western Culture: adrift and dying of thirst for God . . . when the entire earth is full of the Water of Life.

It is reported that my town, New Canaan, one of the most beautiful in New England, has one of the highest per capita incomes of any city in Connecticut. We have some 18,000 residents and some 16,000 vehicles—a car or Hummer for nearly every man, woman, and child in our town.

Still, with what amounts to an Amazon River of spiritual life surging all around us in nature, we are secular sailors, dying of thirst. As the Kalahari Bushmen put it, we have "lost our souls." Created to "walk again with the moon and the stars," many of us are content with a stock portfolio and an SUV.

Increasingly, I will be speaking with someone around town, and they will say something like, "I don't go to church very often. I guess you could say I'm not very religious. But I am a very spiritual person. I experience God all the time . . . just not in church." I believe them, for the most part. Even our churches have lost their way. Something happened to us in our growing up, as individuals and as societies. And it was not healthy. I would postulate that most of us would say that our earliest memories of life and nature were filled with wonder and excitement—even awe. Remember your joy at first listening to the waters of a river or a rainfall, or lying in the wet grass, feeling it, smelling it, becoming one with the earth and the grass, and you, or watching the sunlight dapple through the leaves, or talking with a puppy or a hamster, or a baby bird, or hearing God speak in the thunder?

But how long did that 'natural spirituality' last once you got into Sunday School or Church? Let alone University or the Corporate Culture? Once upon a time, we communed with God in nature. We were "at one" with our fellow inhabitants of earth and the earth itself. What do we do with Creation these days, other than to buy it, develop it, force it to work for us, "comodify" it, sell shares in it, and occasionally remember to thank God for it? What happened to our relationship with nature and nature's God? Have we not, for the most part, been "led to think that spirituality is about looking away from life, so that the Church is distanced from the world, and spirit is almost entirely divorced from the matter of our bodies, our lives and the world?"[34]

The longer I live, the deeper I long for a spirituality that seeks God by looking toward the heart of life, not away from it. As Philip Newell, former warden of the Iona Abby puts it, "God is the Life of the world and not merely some religious aspect of it. To listen for God is to listen deep within ourselves, including deep within the collective life and consciousness of the world."[35]

If any religious group should remember this, it is the Presbyterians, who can trace their lineage back to the Western Isles of Scotland and their Celtic heritage. But if any religious group has forgotten their intimate ties with Creation, it is the Presbyterian descendants of Calvin and Knox.

Our ancestors before them had a name for the lights of the skies, the sun and moon and stars. They were called "graces," the spiritual coming through the physical. God was seen as the Life within all life, not just as the Creator who set life in motion from afar. The image of God was believed to be at the heart of all people, not just the baptized or the chosen. The elements of the earth were expressions of God's grace and goodness, as were the ordinary and the everyday experiences of life. All of life was sacramental and a "means of grace"—not just the writings and rituals of institutional religion.

When St. Paul preached the resurrected Christ to those philosophers on Mars Hill in Athens, he took for granted their natural spiritual connection with creation and affirmed it. "For, as your own poets have said, 'in God [and by God] we live and move and have our being.'" In Paul's thinking, God not only "makes" things, but makes them holy and sustains their existence at every moment. The Greek's problem was that their Natural Theology had no room for Jesus (nor any other human embodiment of the Sacred). Our American problem is that our Jesus Theology has no room for nature.

Many of the great "Prayers of Creation" can be traced back to the monastic community of St. Columba on the tiny island of Iona, Scotland, from the 6th century CE. That rugged, misty isle has been called "a thin place," where it is said that "the shafts of divine light" seem to penetrate "the thin veil dividing heaven and earth."

"The world is charged with the grandeur of God."[36] Not only with grandeur, but with strength, courage, love, compassion, beauty, and blessedness as well. Yes, there is also violence, disease, and death in nature. But it is constantly overshadowed by goodness and life. The whole of Creation is brim-full of the Divine Presence.

So I encourage you to keep an open mind and heart as we seek together to develop an inner ear for God. It may be a stretch for some of our favorite "orthodox" beliefs and perspectives, but at the end of the day, a person needs to be true to their own inner heartbeat of love, goodness, and compassion.

I believe that we can look to Creation, as well as the Scriptures and our faith communities, to experience the living Word of God for us today. When we listen closely enough, we can hear the Heartbeat of God in the Heart of the World. All we need do is to lower our buckets deeply into the mouth of the Amazon.

The Reverend George MacLeod, the great Scottish Presbyterian minister and founder of the Iona Community, calls us back to this fundamental unity of all things:

> *Invisible we see you, Christ above us,*
> *With earthly eyes we see above us clouds or sunshine,*
> *But with the eye of faith we know you reign:*
> *instinct in the sun ray,*
> *speaking in the storm,*
> *warming and moving all creation,*
> *Christ above us . . . .*

> *With earthly eyes we see beneath us stones and dust and dross,*
> *Fit subjects for the analyst's table.*
> *But with the eye of faith, we know You uphold.*
> *In You all things consist and hang together:*
> *The very atom is light energy,*
> *The grass is vibrant,*
> *The rocks pulsate.*

> *All is in flux; turn but a stone and an angel moves.*
> *Underneath are the everlasting arms.*
> *Unknowable we know you, Christ beneath us . . .* [37]

Amen!

CHAPTER 8

DISCOVERING
THE PRIMEVAL POOL

"They that go down to the sea in ships,

that do business in great waters:

These see the works of the Lord,

And his wonders in the deep."

Psalm CVII, v. 23-24

"He that will learn to pray

let him go to sea."

George Herbert, English Divine

Once upon a time in the Far North there lived a young man with the heart of an explorer. For as long as he could recall he had pondered the question of being. Intrigued by the things he could see and touch as well as the fact of his inner being, he wondered, "Why is there *something* and not *nothing*?" Day and night the question plagued him until he could find no rest.

Then one day the matriarch of the village told him that the answer to his question lay at the heart of the primeval forest. In the center of the forest was a pool, and the waters of the pool held the answer to the Mystery of Being. So the brave seeker set out to find the forest and discover the pool.

After years of searching he found the enchanted forest, but there were no pathways into its heart. So another decade passed before, at last, he found his way to the center of the vast wood. One day to his surprise he happened upon a clearing in the depth of the forest. At the center of the clearing lay a large, bubbling pool, and beside the pool sat a bearded old man.

Filled with questions, the brave explorer approached the old man eagerly, but before he could speak, the ancient one silently motioned him into the pool and then joined him. There he gently took the young man in his arms and thrust him under the water. Coming up out of the water his eyes were opened; now he knew the reason for his being; now he knew why there was *something* and not *nothing*.

The encounter with the Mystery of Being changed his heart, and the explorer wished to help his friends journey to the forest, discover the pool, and be immersed in its transforming waters. For a time the explorer clearly marked the pathways from the edges into the center of the primeval forest so others could find their way to the Mystery.

With his work completed it was, at last, time to return home and share with his village the wonderful news of his discovery. One after another said, "Tell us the meaning of Being. Share with us the Mystery!"

But the explorer repeatedly urged, "Go and find out for yourselves!" Knowing he could never tell the Mystery, he made a map of the primeval forest indicating the various pathways he had marked into the center. The villagers pounced on the map, framing it and hanging it prominently in the town hall. Each demanded for themselves a personal copy of the map. They even boasted to the neighboring village about their new possession.

But none of the folk in the explorer's village ever made the journey to the primeval forest; not one ever plunged into the pool; so none of them ever found the meaning of the Mystery. It was enough for them to know that someone had made the journey. They felt secure owning a map.[38]

Millions of times each day around the world, in hundreds of languages, from all types of human beings in all conditions of life, one prayer rises up to the One who is the Mystery of Being. There is not a single moment at any time of day or night when it is not being repeated somewhere: a great choral symphony rising from God's people around the world. It has many names: The "Our Father," "The Jesus Prayer," and "The Lord's Prayer."

Yet, as rich and sublime as this prayer is, there is the danger of using it as a magic talisman rather than a sacred path, a "hitching post" rather than a "signpost," a personal possession rather than a universal map. If just saying it would make it true, then why, for the past 2,000 years, have the "kingdoms of this world" not become "the kingdoms of our God"?

Napoleon once asked, "Do you wish to see that which is really sublime?" and answered his own question: "Repeat the Lord's Prayer." But apparently that was all he did; he only repeated it. He memorized it and mastered it and memorialized it. But he was not changed by it.

Whether it is a bronze tablet of the Ten Commandments hung in a courtroom or a framed manuscript of The Lord's Prayer hung in a classroom, the reality is the same. The Mystery which transforms us and the world is not ours to possess or control. At best, like the young explorer, all we can do is to immerse ourselves into the presence of the One to whom these things point.

William Temple said, "If you have a false idea of God, the more religious you are, the worse it is for you—it were better for you to be an atheist."

The Lord's Prayer came in answer to a prayer. Jesus' disciples admitted that they did not know how to pray. In John's gospel, they ask Jesus, "Lord, teach us to pray." That sounds like a noble thing, doesn't it? "Please teach us to pray." There is, however, the issue of motive. Why? They had each seen Jesus pray to his God and then speak and act with power and authority. What did he know that they did not?

Jesus' first instruction was a comparison to the common practice of the day. At 3:00 p.m. every afternoon, it was required of all Jews that they stop what they were doing and offer prayers. Public prayer in the synagogue was normal and appropriate. Public prayer in the center of a wide and busy street was not normal, nor appropriate. Jesus' allusion to going into one's closet to pray was not intended to be taken literally. He was not opposed to public prayer in the synagogue, only to making a spectacle of one's piety in public—praying to people, not to God.

How did Matthew and the early community of Jesus remember his teachings about prayer? Well, for starters, they realized that he was not saying anything they had not heard before in their religious tradition. Jesus and his early followers were religious Jews. They had been brought up as children to think of God not just as the Father of their Nation, but of the world. Aware of it or not, they worshipped a non-parochial God who was bigger than themselves, their culture, or even their religion.

When we begin our prayers to God as "Our Father," we go far beyond the old paternalistic, male chauvinism of our traditions. Mentally, we know that God is not a man, but rather a Divine Parent, the source of all life. In our worship services we often pray to "our *Father/Mother* God," and always sing the Doxology, "Praise God from whom all blessings flow, praise God all creatures here below, Praise God above ye heavenly host, *Creator, Christ, and Holy Ghost.*"

Dante said that "once the human soul ceases saying 'me' and 'mine,' but rather 'our' and ours,' then they have made the transition to the truly spiritual life. Christianity, like its mother religion, Judaism, and its kindred religion, Islam, is always personal, but never private. It connects us intimately to God and our neighbor. The Aramaic word Jesus originally spoke is "Abba," literally meaning "Daddy," a term of affection and respect.

This alone can change the world.

A decade ago the headlines read, "Cease-Fire in Macedonia Stops the Guns But Not the Ethnic Distrust and Bitterness."[39] How do you stop the ethnic distrust and bitterness?

Can you imagine what might happen if every family of the two major ethnic groups in Macedonia—the Slavic Macedonians (who are mostly Orthodox Christians) and the Albanians (who are mostly Muslims)—began and ended each day with humble prayers to their common "Father," praying as a part of an intimate family circle? Both of them claim Abraham as their spiritual father and Abraham's God as their own God. Can you imagine either of them praying for peace to "Our Daddy, who art in heaven...," and then going out to bomb, or shoot or gas their own brothers and sisters? Impossible!

But the Lord's Prayer is not just for "those people over there." It is for us here as well. How many times do we hear the question from our children, "Why are there so many poor people in the world?" Clearly, it is not easy to give your child a simple answer to that question. There are many reasons. Yet we must never dodge the essential one: The "haves" forgot that they and the "have-nots" are children of one Father. Lines of economic greed find no place in the love of the Lord's Prayer. It is the same with nationalism. There are no enemy aliens in this spiritual temple of prayer; every person is a member of the same family. We may not be "our brother's keeper," but we are always "our brother's brother," "our sister's sister."

How can there be a "Brotherhood and Sisterhood of Humanity" without the "Fatherhood" or "Parenthood" of God? "Father" was not a Jewish title for God. It was first of all Jesus' word for his own relation to God. He then included his disciples and all human beings in this relationship. As children of the One God, we are all "brothers and sisters," not only of one another but also of Jesus, sharing his intimate, personal relationship with God.

An individual cannot be complete without the "beloved community" of brothers and sisters in their faith community and in the whole family of races, cultures, and nations. The God to whom we pray is too big to fit into any one religion, creed, or country.

So, how do we make our way through the thick woods and undergrowth of the enchanted forest? The safest pathways into the Mystery of Life have been identified, marked, and tested by millions of previous pilgrims. The movements of the Lord's Prayer can be trusted to lead us into God. As Augustine prayed, "Thou hast made us for thyself, O God, and our hearts are restless until they rest in thee."

Remember the ancient mariner, in the Coleridge poem? He was spiritually "dead in the water" and his vessel held in a death-like trance until he prayed with compassion for all of God's creatures, not just for himself. How true it is that, "He prayeth best who loveth best."[40]

To pray and live The Lord's Prayer is to jump into the clear, bubbling embrace of God, and to join hearts and hands with millions of others in moving world history at its central junctures.

CHAPTER 9

A FINGER POINTING TO THE MOON

"It is time we steered by the stars,
not by the lights of each passing ship."
—GENERAL OMAR BRADLEY

"For us as Christians, God is defined by Jesus,
*but not **confined** to Jesus."*
—WILLIAM SLOANE COFFIN, JR.

Robert Capon, Episcopal priest, novelist, and gourmet chef, contrasts Jesus with Clark Kent: "The true paradigm of the ordinary American view of Jesus is Superman: 'Faster than a speeding bullet, more powerful than a locomotive, able to leap tall buildings in a single bound. It's Superman! Strange visitor from another planet, who came to earth with powers and abilities far beyond those of mortal men, and who, disguised as Clark Kent, mild-mannered reporter for a great metropolitan newspaper, fights a never ending battle for truth, justice and the American Way.'

"If that isn't popular Christology, I'll eat my hat," says Capon. Jesus—gently, meek and mild, but with secret, souped-up, more-than-human insides—bumbles around for thirty-three years, nearly gets himself done in for good by the Kryptonite Kross, but at the last minute, struggles into the phone booth of the Empty Tomb, changes into his Easter suit and with a single bound, leaps back up to the planet Heaven. It's got it all—including, just so you shouldn't miss the lesson, kiddies: *He never once touches Lois Lane.*"[41]

No historical figure has generated more commentary and controversy than Jesus of Nazareth. Such attention is extraordinary in light of the fact that his career lasted at most only a few years and his activities were confined to his own homeland. Yet, the brief life and narrowly focused ministry of this first century Palestinian Jew became the basis for what is now a religion of universal appeal with the largest number of followers in the world.

"He was and is such a man of mystery," writes theologian Paul Laughlin—"a person who is rarely visible, and only in soft focus. He left no writings, apparently spoke and taught in an oblique and ambiguous style that puzzled even his closest followers, and — despite later claims to the contrary—founded no institution and left no clear agenda or program to be followed in his name. Complicating the situation is the fact that most of what we know about Jesus is based on New Testament writings that were composed long after the fact, are very sketchy and often contradictory, and are already biased by several layers of Christian belief, interpretation, and intent . . .

It is no wonder, then, that successive generations have remembered this man in a variety of ways, refashioning him time and again in their own images. He has been portrayed as everything from a simple rabbi to a deluded religious fanatic to a revolutionary zealot to the redeemer of all humanity. He has been reconceived in every culture and age according to its own standards and values, hopes and aspirations, and by countless individuals in light of their own predispositions, preferences, and prejudices. Historians of Christianity and Christian thought have shown again and again how views of and beliefs about Jesus have grown, developed, changed, and been codified (and sometimes condemned) in doctrines and dogmas over the centuries."[42]

A major revisioning of Christianity is underway today, especially in the United States. When I use the term, "revisioning," what I mean to describe is a faithful attempt on the part of many today to "re-vision," to attempt "to see again," the meanings of Jesus for our life and faith together. Christianity is no longer a matter of *believing* the right things about God and Jesus as it been for nearly 1,800 years, but about *living in relationship* with the Living Christ within the community of faith. In other words, faith is not so much a *noun* as it is a *verb*.

The Bible and the Christian tradition are "mediators of the sacred," like signposts pointing to something beyond themselves. They do not fully reveal God to us, but rather point us in the direction of God. We are not meant to believe in them, but rather to trust in that to which they point. "Believing in Jesus does not mean believing doctrines about him," as Marcus Borg puts it. "Rather, it means to give one's heart, one's self at it deepest level, to . . . the living Lord."

The unique affirmation of Christianity is that, unlike any other of the world's major religions, we find the revelation of God to us primarily in a *person*, not in a creed or a sacred writing. In Judaism and Islam, Moses and Muhammad are receivers of revelation, but God is not revealed in them fully as persons. Rather, God is revealed in the teachings of the Torah and the Qur'an. So it is in

Buddhism. The revelation of God is not the Buddha as a person, but rather the Buddha's teachings which disclose the path to enlightenment and compassion. This does not make Christianity superior to other religions, but it does make it unique.

The Christian tradition speaks of Jesus as 'fully God and fully man.' What does this mean? I like the way Borg puts it: "This is the central meaning of incarnation: Jesus is what can be seen of God embodied in a human life. He is the revelation, the incarnation, of God's character and passion—of what God is like and of what God is most passionate about. He shows us the heart of God . . . . Jesus is more central than the Bible; when they disagree, Jesus wins."[43]

In Jesus, "the Word became flesh and lived among us, full of grace and truth." This high statement of Jesus' full humanity and full divinity, written by the author of the Gospel of John at the end of the 1st century, did not take on its present meaning until 400 years after Jesus' death and resurrection. Our religion's orthodox Christological formula (what might be called "The *Archetypal Christ*") was finally produced by the Council of Chalcedon in 451 Common Era. The person of Jesus the Christ was said to be both fully God and fully human, two complete natures seamlessly fused—yet absolutely unmixed— in one unique person.

But that was not what Jesus' followers thought of him. That composite evolved over hundreds of years from three other master images. First there was the *"The Historical Jesus."* This is what we think might be the actual sayings and actions of Jesus (reported in Mark's Gospel around 40 CE) from the beginning of his public ministry around 29 CE, until his death just a few years later. This image was followed by *"The Narrative Jesus."* These are the teachings, attitudes, deeds, and life drama of Jesus expressed in the stories of Jesus told and retold in various ways by generations of his early followers, mostly recorded in Matthew and Luke, around 70-85 CE. Finally there was *"The Sacred Christ,"* intimations of Jesus' divinity mostly from the high Christology of Paul, around 50 CE, and John, around 100 CE.

Thinking about how these various images of Jesus came to be is important not only because it helps us remember that Jesus was many things to many people, but also because it reminds us that he continues to be that for people today. Those who tend to value *intellect and reason*, for example, take a great deal of interest in Mark's Historical Jesus. The *ethically-oriented* tend to concentrate more on the moral teachings of Matthew and Luke's Narrative Jesus. The *devotionally-focused* Christian tends to gravitate toward John's Sacred Christ. While the *mystical believer* might focus primarily on the Archetypal Christ of the Chalcedonian formulation.[44]

Christians claim that something happens to us when we follow Jesus, just as something happened to the followers of Jesus in his own day. What did they see in Jesus?

New Testament scholar Walter Wink puts it this way: "They saw a human being fully alive, and for them, such life carried divine power and authority. But more important, this way of being fully and freely human 'had now entered the heart of reality as a catalyst in human transformation. Like a bell that reverberates to the core of our being [Jesus, the incarnate Word of God], the [one, fully] Human Being is, as it were, an invitation to become the fullness of who we are. And with the invitation comes the power to do it.'"[45]

Personally speaking, Jesus is the *heart* of my faith. In Jesus, God speaks God's word to me. God's spirit becomes incarnate—"enfleshed"—in my flesh and blood. In him, all of life is sacred. As Gilbert Friend Jones puts it, "Jesus laughed, wept, scolded, reasoned, argued, cajoled, loved deeply, suffered disappointment, studied, worshiped, prayed intensely, faced despair, celebrated, stayed up late at night, ate, drank, partied, and healed people."

"'You want to experience the Realm of God?' Jesus asked. And he gave us a way . . . . He said *repent*, take responsibility for what is wrong in your life and change the course; *trust* the universe, it will always provide; *forgive*, and be free from your demons; free yourself from the *judgment* of others; *love* compassionately and abundantly; have a *generous heart* with your time and money; do not be afraid to *take a costly stand for the justice* of the less privi-leged; and for God's sake never miss an opportunity to *celebrate and give thanks* for the gift of life."[46]

CHAPTER 10

THE CELTIC SECRET

*"Whose dwelling is the light
of the setting sun."*

—WILLIAM WORDSWORTH

"God saw everything that God had created,
and indeed, it was very good."
GENESIS 1:31

A lot of people do not agree with God on this issue. They
have been taught by their church that at the heart of it, the
whole creation (including humanity) is evil, sinful, no
good, and rotten to the core. They love words like *"original sin"*
and *"total depravity."* They sing with the slave-trader John Newton,
"Amazing grace, how sweet the sound, that saved a *wretch* like
me," as though his personal demons were their own. They quote
the Psalmist, "In *sin* did my mother conceive me." Or the prophet,
"All our righteousness is as *filthy rags*." Or Paul when he writes, we
are *"dead* in trespasses and sins "O *wretched man* that I am, who
shall deliver me?" It is like the dour woman who, when she was
told to "Have a nice day!" said, "No thank you, I have other plans!"

There is a visual aid which used to be used in "Released Time
Bible Groups" during public school hours to evangelize children (a
concept which I now find contemptible). It was called "The
Wordless Book." It contained no words; only five colored pages.
Each had a spiritual meaning. The first page was black. The teacher
was to show it to the child and tell him or her that this is because
the child's heart is black with sin. The second was red. This is
because Jesus shed his blood to cover our black hearts. The third
was white. This is because, if we believe in Jesus, our hearts are
white as snow. The forth was green. Now we can grow in our faith.
And the fifth was gold; until at last we walk the streets of gold in
heaven. I had to be taught to believe that. Thank God I never
learned the lesson.

In the movie, *The Crying Game*, the captive says to the captor
of the Irish Republican Army, "There is a story of a frog and a scorpion. The frog carries the scorpion across a river on its back.
Halfway across the scorpion stings the frog and the frog asks why.
The scorpion replies, 'Because it's my nature.'"

That is the question for all of us. Are we, in our deepest beings, the *Image of God* or the *Image of Evil*? Are we so depraved that, as Augustine put it, we are "not able not to sin"?

There is a story of Martin Luther as a young man. He was so guilt-ridden by his sins that, if it were possible, he would have gone to confession every hour. On most nights Luther slept well, but he even felt guilty about that, thinking, "Here am I, sinful as I am, having a good night's sleep." So he would confess that the next day. One day the older priest to whom Luther went for confession said to him, "Martin, either find a new sin and commit it, or quit coming to see me!" This may well have been the birthplace of his later motto: *"If you must sin, Sin Boldly!"*

This brings to mind what Garrison Keillor said about growing up Lutheran in Lake Woebegone: "I'm not sure I'm in favor of repentance," he said. "Sinners are the ones who get the work done. A strong sense of personal guilt is what makes people willing to serve on church committees!"

Celtic spirituality, the spirituality of our Irish and Scottish ancestors, is quite different from our Western theology handed down to us from Augustine. Augustinian Christianity views *sin as the basic problem*. Because Adam and Eve bit into the forbidden fruit and broke God's law, they were pronounced guilty. And this *"original sin"* transmits guilt to every generation after them. Because we are inherently sinful, as the theory goes, we cannot through our own effort set things right between ourselves and God. God sent Jesus to pay the price we could not pay for our sin. His death on the cross *"paid the price of our redemption."* Salvation comes in *believing* this.

"In Celtic Christianity, as in Eastern Orthodoxy, the *basic problem is not sin but death.* God made creation in order to love it and receive love in return. But, since love cannot be commanded, God gives humans a choice . . . . To eat of that tree was to choose what God had not blessed or made life-giving; it was to choose death. Because they chose the tree, death entered creation, and no action on our part can change that. But Jesus came, did battle with the forces of death, and conquered death—for all humanity."[47]

Salvation comes in *acting as though* life is actually more powerful than death.

In Augustinian theology, because we are inherently evil, we are unable to make the right choices. In Celtic spirituality, God has given each of us the ability to choose good or evil, to love or reject God. Every day is an opportunity to say "yes" to God, who is all around us and deep within us. All of nature is filled with God's grace [and goodness] and with saints and angels assisting us in our choice. Deep within us, no matter how we degrade ourselves or harm others, the image of God remains, moving us to choose life."[48]

Western Christianity is focused on *"original sin."* Celtic Christianity is focused on *"original blessing."* "If we take the universe to be about twenty billion years old, as scientists are advising us to do, then sin of the human variety is about four million years old, since that is how long humans have been around. But creation is 19 billion, 996 million years older! . . .Nineteen billion years before there was any sin on earth, there was blessing."[49]

"Original sin" is not found in the Bible. As 20th Century Jewish prophet Elie Wiesel points out, "The concept of *"original sin"* is alien to Jewish tradition."[50] You and I are born into a broken, torn and sinful world, to be sure. "But we do not enter as blotches on existence, as sinful creatures, we bust into the world as *"original blessings."*[51]

When our son, Sean, was born, I stood in the hallway of the neo-natal care unit while the nurse held him up to the glass and unwrapped and counted out each of his fingers and each of his toes, and showed me that his arms and legs worked, and that his little head bobbed from side to side. What I saw was the awesome ultimate of beauty and goodness. What I later held in my arms was not an ugly black heart of "original sin." What I cradled in my arms was a creation of God's image and likeness. It was an *"original blessing."*

"No one believed in *"original sin"* until Augustine. 'Original sin' is an idea that [he] developed late in his life and, to his credit, it was not all that significant in his theology either. Sad to say, however, original sin grew to become a starting point for Western religion's flight from nature, creation, and the God of creation."[52]

For Augustine, sin was transmitted sexually. He viewed the begetting of children and all lovemaking as at least venially sinful because it was carnal and because one "lost control" in passion (Thanks be to God, I say!). For the Celts, on the other hand, love, desire, and passion has its origin in the Creator's love for creation and in our parents love and desire for one another.

When Bev and I attended our goddaughter's graduation from Kindergarten into First Grade (at a supposedly Christian school), the preacher told the children and their parents that all of us are born as dung into the compost heap of life. But all is not lost, he said, because God can create carrots out of the dredges of garbage. Mandie, our goddaughter, was five years old! (Which is one of the strong reasons I support public education!)

Those images stay with us. As William Eckhardt has demonstrated in his substantial study on the psychology of compassion, he never found a "compassionate adult who did not have a radical trust in human nature."[53]

That school principal/preacher got his theological biology from Augustine. Augustine taught that every child is born depraved and bound for perdition.

On the other side of the aisle in this issue (in the Celtic corner) is Pelagius, the much-maligned fourth-century British Christian, who maintained that the image of God can be seen in every newborn child and that, although obscured by sin, it exists at the heart of every person, waiting to be released through the grace of God. Pelagius was branded a heretic for these views and although exonerated by the Pope, he was condemned by Augustine and the African bishops, banished from Rome, and excommunicated from the Church.

Celtic spirituality "offers an alternative to the guilt package of Augustine. In understanding God as granting us the right to say 'yes' or 'no' and honoring our choice, it views us not as forever [sinful] children, 'worms,' depraved, guilty, and incapable of choosing good, but as created good, intrinsically worthy of God's favor, and able to love God as God created us to do."[54] One image pictures us as bent and broken, helpless and powerless victims being lifted up out of a pit. The other pictures us as created of wind and fire on a mountain top, ready to soar with the eagles and change the world.

For those of us who are still struggling with a negative self-image, unable to believe that we are goodness, struggling to crawl out of what we imagine to be the compost heap of life, the good news is that we are created in the very image of God. If there is no goodness in us, there is no goodness in God. Our prayer is not to be saved from all of the negative within and around us, but to live into the promise of all we were created to be—sons and daughters of the earth, birthed by the God of the Universe, and nurtured by the mothering Spirit of Divine Love.

And so I pray not that you might become someone else, but that you might become the person you were created to be. In the words of a Celtic prayer,

> *May God make safe to you each step,*
> *May God make open to you each pass,*
> *May God make clear to you each road,*
> *And may He take you in the clasp of*
> *His own two hands.*[55]

CHAPTER 11

THE MEANING OF JESUS' LIFE AND DEATH

"All streams run to the sea,

but the sea is not full;

to the place where the streams flow,

there they continue to flow."

— ECCLESIASTES 1:7

2007 was an unusual year for the three Abrahamic religions. Rosh Hashanah, the Jewish New Year, Ramadan, Islam's holy month, and the Christian celebration of World Communion Sunday were each celebrated concurrently.

My friend, Dr. Kareem Adeeb, President of the American Institute for Islamic and Arabic Studies in Stamford, Connecticut, tells me that Muslims believe that in 610 CE, Allah revealed the first verses of the sacred text of the Qu'ran to Mohammad during Ramadan, the ninth month of the Muslim calendar. This month of atonement for sins is named for the Arabic word which means "to pulverize." The entire month is dedicated to pulverizing sins away, he says. Ramadan is not just fasting from food and water, but adult Muslims must also give to the poor and refrain from smoking and sex between sunrise and sunset.

This raises the issue: What is the meaning of Jesus' life and death for a Christian's salvation?

When a person joins The Presbyterian Church (USA)—the denomination in which I am a minister—they are asked the question: "Do you trust in Jesus Christ as your Lord and Savior?" This is the most common historic formulation of Christian faith. By saying *"trust in"* rather than *"believe in"* Jesus Christ, we affirm that we see Christianity as a "way," not a "system of intellectual beliefs." *Belief* suggests an access to God through knowledge. *Trust* suggests an access to God through relationship.

So right from the start, we need to be clear that one does not "become a Christian," or "declare oneself to be a Christian," by believing certain things about God, Jesus, the Bible, theology, ethics, politics, social betterment, or whatever. "The Way" of the Christian religion is a "way of life," a way of being human in an inhumane world, of living in love not hate, of faith not fear, of hope not despair, of forgiveness not revenge.

So what does it mean to "trust in Jesus Christ as one's Lord and Savior"? Well, the titles used of Jesus, "Lord" and "Savior," are used differently in different situations and require some contextual understanding.

In Jesus' day the title "Lord" was a statement of authority. It was commonly used of the Roman Emperor. It meant that the title-bearer was in fact the Lord of the Realm, the Supreme Commander, and the one who was to be served by all others who were his vassals. The Emperor was also revered as God, or as the Son of God, or as God's incarnation on the earth.

The title, "Lord," was a statement of allegiance. For a Christian to declare the Lordship of Jesus rather than the Lordship of Caesar was a profound and costly commitment. It meant than Caesar was not the ultimate Lord of the Realm. This in itself was often a self-proclaimed death sentence. Thousands of people in the first few hundred years of the Christian religion were ostracized or killed by the government because they asserted that Jesus is Lord, not Caesar, nor any earthly ruler.

To declare in the 21st century CE that "Jesus is Lord" is to declare that President George W. Bush is not Lord, and that Ban Ki-moon, Secretary-General of the United Nations, is not Lord, nor is any government or institution.

To my knowledge, no one was killed because they asserted that Jesus was their Savior. The title "Savior" was used by a number of Jesus early followers, mostly those of Jesus' race who understood its symbolic meaning within the Jewish sacrificial system in which on a prescribed day a pure lamb (or other animal) was slain and its blood poured on the temple alter—reenacting the redemption story of the blood of the lamb which was painted on the doorposts of Jewish homes in Egypt during the Passover hundreds of years before.

The whole idea of a sacrificial system requiring a blood sacrifice is strange to most 21st century Christians. Few human beings today can relate to the necessity of a "blood offering" in order to be right with God. While some Christians understand Jesus' death as payment (or ransom) to God, the "final sacrifice" for human sin, they don't really want to push that idea too far, since it makes God out to be an angry deity, despising what God had created, and requiring the shedding of blood for some sort of divine satisfaction.

I find the very idea of a God who would demand to be assuaged by human or animal sacrifice or by killing or war to be demonic, sadistic, and totally abhorrent. Further, I believe that that kind of bad theology is more dangerous now than ever before in our world of religious absolutism and religious violence—when the entire world is a hair-trigger away from self-annihilation . . . and those triggers are being held by religious zealots of all stripes. Frankly, it is not that far a leap from believing in that kind of violent God to believing that that same God requires his "true believers" to do the same in slaying infidels in the name of all that is Holy.

In the Christian Scriptures the Apostle Paul saw a clear parallel between the figures of Adam and Christ. Adam had been disobedient, and thus had brought sin and death and condemnation into the world; Christ been obedient, and consequently had brought righteousness, life, and acquittal. (Romans 5:12-19) Paul was certain that the death of Jesus was the gracious act of God that brought atonement, but *how* that happened was not as clear to Paul.

As a result, successions of theories of atonement were developed as far back as the Middle Ages. Five of them rose to the top:

"One, the *satisfaction theory*, was derived from ancient Jewish ritual practices and thus regarded Christ as a sacrifice to God that appeased the deity, who had been so offended by human sin.

"Another, the *substitution theory*, held that the death of Jesus was not so much a sacrifice as a payment to God for the debt owed by humanity by virtue of sin.

"Yet another, the *ransom theory*, reasoned that sinfulness had put humanity on the Devil's 'turf,' and that God had made the payment to Satan necessary to free us.

"A fourth, the *victory theory*, suggested that far from being a payment to the Devil, Christ through his 'obedience unto death' affected a defeat-in-principle over the power of evil.

"Still another, the *moral theory*, held that the real point of Jesus' obedience and death was to provide an example for humanity to follow."[56]

I do not accept what has been called "Atonement Theology," which assumes that since we are fallen humanity, there had to be a time when we were not fallen. I do not believe that there ever was a *"state of innocence"* for the human race. The Genesis story is mythological, not factual. We are now, and have always been, good and bad, capable of great good and terrible evil. We do not need to be rescued, except from ourselves (when we become our own worst enemy). I understand the process of life to be evolutionary. We are still incomplete human beings who do not need to be *"saved," but rather* to be *"empowered"* to become all that we can be for the sake of others and the world.

The way many progressive Christians today understand "Jesus as Savior" is not as a type of pagan sacrificial offering, but rather as a metaphor for God through Jesus enlightening and enabling us to become what he was, and what we can hope to become, which is "fully human" in the divine image.

"Jesus Christ was not God's entry into human life . . . . It was this divine involvement in human history, hidden from the beginning . . . that was made manifest in Jesus . . . . In Christ is revealed that the way of God's presence is in incarnation. God acts through the human in ordinary words and gestures, in personal relations." (Gregory Baum)

This, of course, is the same intent as those early followers of Jesus—those who walked with him during his life, who witnessed the absolute grace of his words and actions, who proclaimed his message of unlimited love and inclusion, of healing and reconciliation, and who sought to live his Way after his death. From its beginning, Christianity was about *following Jesus*, not about trying to *figure him out*.

Having said that, we can never forget that, "We Christians participate in the only major religious tradition whose founder was executed by established authority."[57] And that authority was not Religion; it was the State.

Why was Jesus killed? If it was only because of his spiritual connection with a higher power, or because of his extraordinary ability to bring about personal healing, or because of his brilliant philosophical insights into the meaning of life, I doubt that he would have been killed at all. Rather, I believe with Marcus Borg and others that Jesus was killed because of his *politics* and his *courage*—because of his *passion* for embodying God's justice on behalf of those who were being denied it. And I would add, because of his *person*. Never before nor since have human beings seen a fully human person so full of goodness, love, and God as Jesus.

Progressive Christians do not believe that Jesus thought that the purpose of his life, his divine vocation, was to die. As with Martin Luther King, Mahatma Gandhi, Oscar Romero, Stephen Biko, and so many others, Jesus' death was the *consequence* of what he was doing with his life, not the *purpose* of it.

"To seek a new way, a totally different way to tell the Christ-story—if it can be told in a new way—is our only option," declares John Shelby Spong. "The Christian church thus stands in the early years of this new millennium on the threshold of either extinction or a radically new beginning. No other alternative presents itself as a possibility . . . .

What does it mean to have a God-experience? What was the Christ-experience for the disciples and others who knew Jesus? How can you and I touch it, appropriate it, and enter it today, two thousand years later?"[58]

These are the questions with which we must grapple in our time.

CHAPTER 12

SACRIFICIAL LAMB OR ENEMY OF THE STATE?

"And so to the end of history
murder shall breed murder,
always in the name of right and honor and peace,
until at last the gods tire of blood
and create a race that can understand."
—G.B. Shaw, Caesar and Cleopatra

On the morning of September 11, 2001, aerial assaults on the World Trade Center and the Pentagon killed thousands of innocent men and women and left even more innocent children, widows, and widowers forever scarred by their killing. When the diaries and plans of the terrorists were found, it was discovered that the assassins were absolutely convinced that they were on a righteous mission in the service of a holy God who demanded the death of the enemy and their own ultimate sacrifice.

When plastic explosives attached to a Hamas suicide bomber ripped through the gentrified Ben Yehuda shopping mall in Jerusalem in September, 1977, the blast damaged not only lives and property, but also the confidence with which most people viewed the world. When the shy young man grinned into the video camera the day before he was to become a martyr, he proclaimed, "I am doing this for Allah."[59]

"It was a cold February night in 1984 when Rev. Michael Bray and a friend drove a yellow Honda from his home in Bowie to nearby Dover, Delaware. The trunk of the car held a cargo of ominous supplies: a cinder block to break a window, cans of gasoline to pour in and around a building, and rags and matches to ignite the flames . . . . 'Before daybreak,' Bray said, 'the only abortion chamber in Dover was gutted by fire and put out of the business of butchering babies.'" And this was only one of seven such abortion facilities he and two others destroyed. Rev. Bray is a born-again Christian who formed what he called the Reformation Lutheran Church. "Bray is convinced that if there were some dramatic event, such as economic collapse or social chaos, the demonic role of the government would be revealed, and people would have 'the strength and the zeal to take up arms in a revolutionary struggle' . . . to establish a new moral order in America, one based on Biblical law and a spiritual, rather than a secular, social compact . . . . According to Bray, Christianity gives him the right to defend innocent 'unborn children,' . . . even if it involves killing doctors and other clinical staff."[60]

There is a dark alliance between religion and violence. Whether it be "among right-wing Christians in the United States, angry Muslims and Jews in the Middle East, quarrelling Hindus and Muslims in South Asia, [or] indigenous religious communities in Africa and Indonesia . . . . Religion is crucial for these [violent] acts, since it gives moral justifications for killing . . . . Religion often provides the mores and symbols that make possible bloodshed—even catastrophic acts of terrorism."[61]

The very Holy Books that each of our religions hold sacred are filled with images of a violent God. One Biblical scholar has found 600 passages of explicit violence in the Hebrew Bible, 1,000 verses where God's own violent actions of punishment are described, 100 passages where God expressly commands others to kill people, and several stories where God irrationally kills or tries to kill for no apparent reason. Violence . . . is easily the most often mentioned activity in the Hebrew Bible."[62]

Is God really as violent and vile as these Biblical writers say? I say, "Absolutely not! God is not like that." The troubling truth, though, is that our religious absolutism and its violent personal and national zeal are rooted in human images of God which are widespread throughout the Bible. We need to confront and challenge them, not only in the light of modern Biblical scholarship, but in light of Jesus' own faith and Jesus' images of God.

I believe that for Christians, the event we celebrate every Palm Sunday—Jesus' triumphal entry into Jerusalem on the back of a donkey—can be for us a starting point for the end of religion-based terrorism and war. If God is a warrior-king or a blood-thirsty deity, then the final week of Jesus' life makes no sense. But if God is a Being of infinite love and compassion, then Jesus' life and death are, for us, "the way, the truth and the life."

Did Jesus die because he was the Sacrificial Lamb of God "slain from the foundation of the world"? Or did Jesus die because his words and his actions so threatened the powers of institutionalized evil in his day that he was killed by those powers as an 'Enemy of The State'?

I believe that the God whom Jesus reveals refrains from all forms of reprisal. God does not endorse so-called "holy wars" nor so-called "just wars." God does not sanction religions of violence . . . . As 20th-century mystic Simone Weil put it, "The reign of God means the elimination of every form of violence between individuals and nations."

I firmly believe that Jesus was not killed by God's hand, nor by God's plan. Jesus was executed because he was an Enemy of the State. Simply put, Jesus was viewed as a dangerous radical: "too good" for his contemporaries, "too loving" of his enemies, and "too committed" to embodying the non-violent Kingdom of God. In his teaching and his actions, he stood firmly against the institutions, groups, and ideas that powerfully shaped and distorted the religious, economic, and political life of his day.

Directed by Rome and Temple, this oppressive system was responsible for Jesus' death and for the hunger, poverty, violence, and despair that were part of daily life for the vast majority of his contemporaries.

That Domination System in Jesus' day was marked by three characteristics:

1. A politics of oppression,
2. An economics of exploitation, and
3. A religion of legitimation.[63]

I believe that the cross of Christ both exposed and began to defeat the powers of the Domination System that kept people broken, oppressed, and powerless. In Jesus' death and resurrection, God initiated the ultimate defeat of the principalities and powers of the universe that have so long held humankind in bondage.

The crucifixion of Jesus exposed those powers. The resurrection of Jesus counters the system's ultimate sanction that is death. Clearly, the death and resurrection of Christ is not the end of evil, violence, or injustice—they still exist. The death of Jesus neither transforms them nor redeems them. In fact, it leaves them largely untouched. What the resurrection of Christ does do is to overturn the world's value system, herald our own resurrection, and free us to challenge evil, violence, and injustice, energized by the presence and power of the Living Christ within us.

How ironic it is today that no pilgrim in Jerusalem can walk the "Via de la Rosa," the "Way of the Cross," because of religious violence. How much better it would be on Palm Sunday if we would begin to follow Jesus' footsteps in our own lives:

- not by endlessly rehearsing and remorsing over our sins,
- not by letting evil win by refusing to confront it with love,
- not by flagellating ourselves for our past mistakes.

But rather,
- by not keeping our mouth shut in the face of wickedness, not by "going along to get along" with the world,
- by not "rolling over and playing dead" to the violence and violation of humanity we see everyday in our homes, our streets, and in our world, and
- by not tacitly supporting the invisible powers of institutional evil and death which parade themselves as Christian.

Let us on Palm Sunday and every day emulate the true "Passion of Christ"—not in his physical death,
but in his refusal to let love die,
in his refusal to let hope die,
in his refusal to let God die,
in his refusal to let the future die.

The truly Christian life springs not from fear, but from a divine passion. "It is the open wound of God in one's own life coming alongside the open wound in the tormented children of the earth."[64]

Jesus kept his head and hopes high by living passionately into his baptism by John in the Jordan River, where he remembered hearing his God say, "You are my beloved son, in whom I am well pleased." Jesus' passion ultimately drove him to love the world to death. Like Jesus, we must not run from who we are created to be. It is not so much that we choose our destiny, as it is that our destiny chooses us.

Søren Kierkegaard once said this age will die, not from sin, but from a lack of passion. Our lack of passion is killing us, and killing Christ's church. We have lost sight of Calvin's image on that seal of dedication: A fervent heart in the palm of an open hand. Beneath the symbol is written: *"I offer my heart to thee, O God, promptly and earnestly."* We need our hearts on fire for God.

Bishop John Spong said it well: "Most churches will die of boredom long before they die of controversy. They are unwilling to risk death in order to engage the search for truth."[65]

Our passion for God's reign of love, truth, and justice on the earth may make us enemies of the state, or enemies of the church, or enemies of the club. But, as John Templeton put it, "The person who has a *why* to live for, can bear with almost any *how*."

Too many nice Christian people *die* before they *live*. How sad! Let's change that. Let's each of us resolve to *live* until we *die*.

And remember, no matter how tough it gets by Friday . . . Sunday's coming!

CHAPTER 13

ONE LESS ROCKET SCIENTIST... ONE MORE WHALE RIDER

"They that go down to the sea in ships,

that do business in great waters

These see the works of the Lord,

and his wonders in the deep."

PSALM CVII, v. 23-24

The college's admissions committee was reviewing applications from high school students for the incoming freshmen class. They plowed through hundreds of student essays on why the writer should be admitted to the school; their eyes glazed over reading about the promise and potential of all of these future presidents, rocket scientists, doctors, and lawyers. But one applicant's essay caught the committee's attention for its surprising lack of pretense. The essay read in part:

"I am not a great student nor am I a leader. You could say that I am incredibly average. I work very hard for the grades I get . . . . For the past three summers, I have worked at a camp for children with cancer. At first, I was terrified that I would say something stupid or I would do something that would add to the pain. I was surprised at how much I enjoyed working with these kids. I have been even more surprised at everything I have learned from them about life and death, about coping with illness and disappointment, about what is really important and good.

"I would like to work with chronically ill and physically challenged children. I would like to pursue a degree in education and psychology so that I might try to give these boys and girls something of what they have given me."

The student's application was immediately put in the "admit" pile. The committee felt that they already had enough presidents and Nobel laureates to choose from; they wanted to make sure they had room for one good, dedicated teacher.[66]

That high school senior knew the difference between a career and a calling. A career seeks to be successful, a calling to be valuable. A calling was once defined by a 17th century Puritan divine as "that whereunto God hath appointed us to serve the common good."

Karen Armstrong, the great student and teacher of the World's Religions, grew up with an innate hunger for God. Having been raised in the Roman Catholic tradition, she felt led to pursue her heart's longing as a nun. In her early 20's she spent seven years in the rigid confines of a strict monastery for women, trying to be good enough, pure enough, and right enough to serve God in the world. In the process she was shattered by a mental and spiritual breakdown. As she describes her spiritual journey in her book, *The Spiral Staircase: My Climb out of Darkness*, her attempts to be the best Christian she could be only exacerbated her sense of guilt and failure. Since that horrific experience, her life has been spent seeking the common spiritual truth and life at the core of the great religions of the world.

Like that high school senior, Karen's goal in life is not so much mastering knowledge as it is making a difference in the world. As Plato said, "What's honored in a country will be cultivated there." Now that we have all this knowledge, what in the world are we going to do with it?

"Religion is not about accepting twenty impossible propositions before breakfast," Armstrong says, "but about doing things that change you. It is a moral aesthetic, an ethical alchemy. If you behave in a certain way you will be transformed. The myths and laws of religion are not true because they conform to some metaphysical, scientific, or historical reality but because they are life enhancing . . . . In the course of my studies, I have discovered that the religious quest is not about discovering "the truth" or "the meaning of life" but about living as intensely as possible here and now . . . . In the past, my own practice of religion had diminished me, whereas true faith, I now believe, should make you more human than before."[67]

I have spoken with Karen about her ardent spiritual quest. And I believe that, although she would undoubtedly deny it, she is a "good shepherd" of disillusioned truth-seekers like herself. Her life's mission, like the best of the Biblical prophets, is not to control the truth, but "to give light to those who sit in darkness and in the shadow of death, to guide our feet into the way of peace."

I commend a wonderful movie to you: "Whale Rider" is about a tribe's search for a strong ruler who can lead its people into a future that their ancestors had only imagined. But, as the story says, "Prophets are not always what you want or what you expect."

"Whale Rider" gets its name from the myth that the Maori people originated in New Zealand as a result of their patriarch riding there many generations ago from "Hawaiki" on the back of a whale. Tradition has it that the first-born son of the chief will be groomed to become the next chief. But his son is not interested. His wife gives birth again, this time to twins, a boy and a girl, but the mother and son die at childbirth, leaving only the daughter, "Pai." But their tradition does not allow a girl to become chief.

As a result, the Maori village had lost its way and its spirit. "There was no gladness when I was born," Pai says. "Everybody was waiting for the firstborn boy, but he died and I didn't. I was not the leader my grandfather was expecting—no one's fault. It just happened."

So one young girl dares to go beyond her fears to confront the past, change the present, and determine the future of her people. While all the boys her age receive instruction about their culture and ancestors, this 12-year-old girl is forced to sneak around, peeking through windows and around corners for the knowledge she seeks. When it comes time to test the young men whom the grandfather has been training, they all fail in their attempt find the whale tooth which had been thrown into the sea. Yet Pai retrieves it, and her uncle recognizes that she is to be the true leader of her tribe.

In the final moments of the film, when a number of whales strangely beach themselves to die on the shore, it is Pai who risks her life by climbing on top of the large lead whale and riding on its back as it swims out to sea into deeper waters. It is only then that her grandfather realizes that their leader has been with them all along but in a form he could not see.

At the end of the story, the whole village launches the whale-boat that had been left unfinished in their despair. In a grand chorus of joy and celebration, Pai leads her people in the rhythm of their life, saying, "I am a part of a long line of chiefs, which go back to the whale rider himself. I am not a prophet, but I know that my people will go forward together, with all of their strength." And so they did.

"I am not a great student, nor am I a leader," wrote that young high school senior. But he was wrong. He was no rocket scientist, yet he had what it took to become a great teacher.

"I was not the leader my grandfather was expecting," said Pai as she began her story. Yet she chose to do what her people most needed and became their true leader.

"God or Nirvana is not an optional extra, tacked on to our human nature," says Karen Armstrong. "Men and women have a potential for the divine, and are not complete unless they realize it within themselves." And she who failed the convent has become a source of spiritual enlightenment for thousands.

Might it be that in these tumultuous days of international fear and disorder, that the world has enough rocket scientists (metaphorically)? Could it be that what we are waiting for is a little child to lead us . . . a whale-rider who will inspire us to leave the beach on which we are dying and swim together toward deeper water?

The promise still awaits fulfillment: "By the tender mercy of our God, the dawn from on high will break upon us, to give light to those who sit in darkness and in the shadow of death, to guide our feet into the way of peace."

As Bill Coffin puts it, "No one is useless in this world who lightens the burden of it for anyone else. And no one makes a greater mistake than those who do nothing because they can only do a little."[68]

Perhaps you are the one who will guide us into that peace.

A HUMANITY BEYOND BORDERS

CHAPTER 14

OUR GATEWAY INTO GOD'S REALM

"The sea has many voices."

— T.S. ELIOT

Duirng World War II the famous American pilot, Captain Eddie Rickenbacker, was flying on a special mission to the Pacific Islands. The plane crashed, and Rickenbacker and his crew were lost at sea for 21 agonizing days. Rickenbacker later wrote of that experience:

"In the beginning many of the men were atheists or agnostics, but at the end of the terrible ordeal each, in his own way, discovered God. Each man found God in the vast, empty loneliness of the ocean. Each man found salvation and strength in prayer, and a community of feeling developed which created a liveliness of human fellowship and worship, and a sense of gentle peace."

Our hearts are strangely warmed, are they not, when we hear Rickenbacker say that "each man, in his own way, discovered God" in his own way.

Yet, if that is the case with those brave souls 60 years ago who "found God in the vast, empty loneliness of the ocean," why is it that so many Christians today cannot believe that the same thing might be true of millions of people around the world who have found God outside of the Christian religion? What makes us think that the only people on earth who have found God, or better, have been found by God, are Christians?

The answer most often given to this question is assumed to come from the lips of Jesus himself: "I am the gate. Whoever enters by me will be saved . . . ." The same point is made in chapter 14 of John, where Jesus is quoted as saying, "I am the way, the truth, and the life, no one comes to the Father except through me."

The truth is that these favorite Bible verses may well not mean what we have assumed they meant. Whether Jesus actually spoke the words (which is doubtful), or the early church created them as consistent with who and what they believed Jesus to be for them in their particular circumstance, is not the critical issue. What is important is that they are linguistic metaphors of faith, figures of speech in which a word denoting one idea is used in place of another to suggest a likeness between them. The writer of John's gospel loves human metaphors: Jesus is the "shepherd," the "bread of life," the "true vine," the "light of the world," the "gate," the "way," the "truth," the "life," etc.

And as metaphors, they are definitively true for Christians today. Jesus is our "gateway" into God's realm, our access into God's reign, God's life. He is our "good shepherd" who cares for us spiritually and provides a safe place for us to be accepted for who we truly are. He "lays down his life for us," as would a good shepherd. He is "the bread of life" and "the wine of joy" for those whose hunger and thirst cannot be satiated by the secularism of our age. He is "the way, the truth, and the life" for us as Christians: our truest and deepest experience of the invisible God.

But to say that this is true for us as Christians is not to say that our language or experience must be true for all people. Marcus Borg tells the story about a sermon preached by a Hindu professor in a Christian seminary several decades ago. The text for the day included the "one way" passage in John 14. Referring to that citation, the Hindu professor said,

"This verse is absolutely true—Jesus is the only way." But the Hindu scholar went on to say, "And that way—of dying to an old way of being and being born into a new way of being—is known in all of the religions of the world." The way of Jesus is a universal way, known to millions who have never heard of Jesus.

The way of Jesus is not about a set of beliefs; it is about a way of life. "Believing in Jesus" does not mean believing certain doctrines about Jesus, "as though one entered new life by believing certain things to be true, or as if the only people who can be saved are those who know the word 'Jesus.' Thinking that way virtually amounts to salvation by syllables. Rather, the way of Jesus is the way of death and resurrection—the path of transition and transformation from an old way of being to a new way of being."[69]

The way of Jesus is the way of nonviolent love over and against violent injustice. The root meaning of the word, "believe" in both Greek and Latin, means, "to give one's heart to." Let's face it, we know more about God's heart than about God's mind. "God is love and those who abide in love abide in God and God in them."[70]

For the Christian, "to believe" really means, "to be-love." That relationship of love transforms us into more and more compassionate beings, "into the likeness of Christ."

We believe that Jesus is "one with God." He is the disclosure of what a life full of God looks like. For Christians, these claims should not be watered down. And we can say, "This is who Jesus is for us" without also saying, "And God is known only in Jesus."[71]

A good many Christians will tell you that they have better access to God than other people. And they demonstrate their convictions by insisting, "We welcome everyone to our church, as long as you're willing to become like us!" That's not a welcome; it's an ambush! "I Love You Just As You Are: Now Change!"

One is reminded of the definition of a "nation" given by the French philosopher, Ernest Renan: "A nation," he says, "is a group of people united by a mistaken view of the past and a hatred of their neighbors."[72] So are many of our churches.

"It is a terrible and dangerous arrogance to believe that you alone are right," said Isaiah Berlin, "that you have a magical eye which sees *the truth* and others cannot be right if they disagree. This makes it certain that there is one way and one only, and that it is worth any amount of suffering (particularly on the part of other people) if only the way prevails."

We have seen this especially since September 11, 2001, as many conservative church leaders have denounced Islam, and even Buddhism and Hinduism as evil religions. In fact, James Mercer, President of the Southern Baptist Convention, was so bold as to urge the millions of Christians in his denomination to join in the celebration of Ramadan by fasting and praying for Muslims' conversions!

Dr. Joseph Hough, former President of Union Theological Seminary, puts the matter clearly: "It is high time that this brand of Christian fundamentalism is called into account for what it is: a distortion of Christianity, resting on an exclusive claim by some Christians that theirs is the only 'true' religion and that all others are evil [or at least inferior]. It is this sort of exclusivist claim that has been at the heart of much of the sorry Christian history of religious wars between Christians, crusades against the Muslims, and continued persecution of the Jews. In these episodes, Christianity has acted as the enemy of peace and goodwill. In our religiously pluralistic nation, such a narrowly triumphalist Christianity echoes the divisive and dangerous fundamentalism that we find so alarming in other religions . . . .

"What is required in this time," Joe says, "is a 'new' Christian theology of religions that moves us beyond tolerance toward genuine respect, or even reverence, for other great religious traditions . . . . What is essential for Christian faith is that we know we have seen the face of God in the face of Jesus Christ. It is not necessary for us to deny that another has seen God in another face at another place or time . . . .

"This does not imply that all religions are equal for me. I am a committed Christian, but I am a Christian who strongly believes that God is working everywhere in exciting ways that I do not yet even know to redeem the world . . . wherever there are faithful practitioners of religious traditions who live with compassion toward other people, who live responsibly toward the world, and who enhance the human community," God is at work.[73]

I love what Bishop Krister Stendahl calls "holy envy." That is, we should try to see something beautiful in what is different from us, something highly desirable, instead of trying to find ways in which we are all the same.

Jesus Christ is my Lord and Savior. I commend him to anyone seeking to know God. Christ is my doorway, my access into God. It is not, perhaps a doorway that everyone can use, and it is certainly not the *only* doorway; but it is *my* doorway.

Further, I concur with Bishop Jack Spong when he says, "My hope is that my brothers and sisters who find Judaism, Islam, Hinduism, Buddhism [or other paths] as their point of entry [into God's realm] . . . will also explore their pathway into God in a similar manner, until they too can escape the limits of their tradition at its depths and, grasping the essence of their system's religious insights, move on to share that essence with me and all the world."

When that happens, "A new day will be born, and Jesus—who crossed every boundary of tribe, prejudice, gender and religion—will be honored by those of us who, as his disciples, have transcended the boundaries of even the religious system that was created to honor him."[74]

I know how hard it is to change cherished ways of thinking. It takes courage to follow one's mind and heart into new truth. I know the struggle that some of you reading this might be going through right now. It has taken me years to come to this place in my spiritual journey. And you and I may not see these things the same way. The important thing is that we give one another the freedom to experience our common faith differently. Because, in the end, it is not what we believe about God that saves us, but what God believes about us.

I think Edwin Markham sums it up best in his poem, "Outwitted":

> *"He drew a circle that shut me out—*
> *heretic, rebel, a thing to flout.*
> *But Love and I had the wit to win.*
> *We drew a circle that took him in."*

May that be true of each of us.

CHAPTER 15

BECOMING WORLD CHRISTIANS

"What we call the beginning is often the end.
And to make an end is to make a beginning.
The end is where we start from . . .

We shall not cease from exploration
And the end of all our exploring
Will be to arrive where we started
And know the place for the first time . . ."
— T.S. ELIOT

S ince the final days of the Second World War, World Communion Sunday has been celebrated in churches throughout the world as a reminder of Christians' solidarity with one another in our quest for peace. In our church we rearrange the pews into four quadrants that Sunday, each facing a center communion table, and literally "come from North, South, East, and West" to join in this Holy Feast.

This past year our special guest on World Communion Sunday was Ms. Hassina Sherjan, a Muslim and Founder and Director of Aid Afghanistan, one woman's vision to build schools for Afghanistani women who are forbidden education under Taliban rule. Hassina's work in this primarily Muslim country is a strong reminder of the unity of our three great religions. Christianity, Judaism and Islam share three essential tenets:

The first is that we are all interconnected in what we call the *"Abrahamic Covenant,"* blessed by God to be a blessing to other nations. The second is that we are each *"monotheistic,"* meaning that we worship One God, rather than many gods. And the third is that each of our religions shares a common mandate *"to love the Lord our God with all our heart, mind, soul, and strength, and to love our neighbor as ourselves."*

One of the Scriptural mandates all three of our religions seek to follow is the first commandment of God to Moses in the Book of Deuteronomy: "I am the Lord your God, who brought you out of the land of Egypt, out of the house of slavery; you shall have no other gods before me."[75]

Having said that, it is important to realize that Deuteronomy is also the one book in the Bible that most explicitly suggests that the Lord may well have stories with other peoples and other religions, not just Jews, Christians and Muslims. "When you look up to the sky and behold the sun and the moon and the stars, the whole heavenly host . . . . These the Lord your God allotted to other peoples everywhere under heaven," says the Bible. "But *you* must not be lured into bowing down to them or serving them" because *"you* the Lord took and brought out of Egypt . . . to be

[God's] very own people . . . ."[76]

In other words, there are many other religions in the world through which God is working. It is a part of what God is about in the universe. But that is God's business, not ours. Our three monotheistic religions have a unique responsibility to follow the truth of God as we know it from our common Sacred Texts. And thereby offer our insights to all the nations.

I believe that as Christians, Muslims, and Jews we have to find a better way for our people to live together harmoniously in the world—especially in the new world of global terror. Surely the God who revealed God's self to us as the Creator of all would have us protect life rather than kill it, to preserve the earth rather than destroy it. Surely our common God would have our nations "confer, not conquer, to discuss, not destroy, to extend olive branches, not . . . missile ranges. The new era already upon us reminds us that God is not mocked: we have to be merciful when we live at each other's mercy . . . ."[77]

What we most need today are World Christians, World Muslims, and World Jews . . . as well as World Buddhists, World Hindus, World Sieks, and the rest. We can no longer afford to remain isolated from one another—either as individuals, religions, or nations.

John Danforth, our American Ambassador to the United Nations from 2004-2005, is an Episcopal clergyman. He is trying to create a new forum of leaders of the world's faiths to help resolve world terrorism. Recently he said, "The focus of the U.N. has been to discuss issues between nations, whereas a lot of the conflict in the world today is not between nations but between nations and individuals who feel they are commanded by God to shoot children and blow up busses." He says there is presently nowhere to bring forward religious grievances and have them publicly discussed and, possibly, reconciled. "What is needed," he said, "is a much stronger voice from the faith community, some kind of place or forum for mediating religious conflict and involving the participation of people of faith."

As a clergyman, Danforth knows the power of religion for good and for evil. Yet he feels that most clergy "are either finessing the issue or ignoring the issue, just getting people to come through their doors and passing the collection plate." He thinks we should be asking the important questions: "What is the relation between government and religion, to what extent is government an arm of religion and, in those countries where it is, to what extent do they provide for the rights of religious minorities? . . . A lot of people think that religion is the answer," he says. "But right now, religion is the problem."[78]

I couldn't agree more. And let's be clear about it, each of our three religions has contributed more than its share of hatred, death, and destruction in the world. As Mark Juergensmeyer puts it in his recent book, *Terror in the Mind of God*, "What makes religious violence particularly savage and relentless is that its perpetrators have placed such religious images of the divine struggle—cosmic war—in the service of worldly political battles. For this reason, acts of religious terror serve not only as tactics in a political strategy but also as evocations of a much larger spiritual confrontation."[79] The faith which was meant to enhance life is now destroying it.

When William Sloane Coffin last preached from our pulpit, his book, *A Passion for the Possible*, had just been published. In it he wrote, "Churches all over the world must see to it that non-violence becomes a strategy not only for individuals and groups, but one taught governments. If arms reductions are to become more likely and wars less so, then new measures have to be devised for conflict resolution. Mediation must become the order of the day."[80]

United we stand, divided we fall. We must work not only for national security, but also for world security, understanding that the security of countries cannot be imagined separately, for none is really secure until all are secure.

What we Christians do on World Communion Sunday in gathering around one worldwide table to envision our oneness in God is not merely for our own good. When we take part in this ancient ritual of peacefully sharing the stuff of life together in a common meal with a common family, the bread and wine we share become symbols of a universal message that surpasses the divisions of nations, the might of missiles, the walls of terror, and the power of fear.

May holy meals like these empower each of us to be agents of hope, reconciliation, and peace in the world. Then shall we be able to join hands and hearts with all good people of other faiths and rejoice with the Psalmist, "How very good . . . it is when kindred live together in unity! For there the Lord ordains his blessing—life forevermore."

May our children live to see that day.

I offer this prayer by my Muslim friend, Dr. Kareem Adeeb, founder of the American Institute of Islamic Arabic Studies in Stamford, Connecticut:

"May God protect us and adorn us with wisdom so that love conquers hatred, tolerance drowns bigotry, moral character over-shadows and eclipses glamour, and wealth is measured by the intrinsic spirituality of a human being rather than by outward materialistic possessions."

Amen.

CHAPTER 16

WHAT THE MUSLIM SAW IN THE MONASTERY

"Whose dwelling is the light
of the setting sun..."
— WILLIAM WORDSWORTH

Ten years ago in Algeria a band of armed Islamic fundamentalists broke into a Trappist monastery in the war-torn village of Tibhirine and took seven Catholic monks hostage. The monks were used as pawns in a murky negotiation to free imprisoned terrorists. Two months later the Archbishop received a macabre message:

"We have cut the throats of the seven monks as we said we would do," read the communiqué. "It happened this morning. May God be praised."

The great irony of the slaughter was that the Tibhirne monastery was known as a place of friendship between Muslims and Christians. For four years both the monastery and the village nearby had been spared the violence that raged in the mountains around them. Napalm, helicopters, and gunfire had become regular accompaniments to the monastic routine of prayer, work, and silence. The monks eventually became victims in a struggle that was not their own—a struggle between Muslims for a more just society—a struggle that had gone horribly wrong and had cost from 60,000 to 100,000 Algerian lives by 1996.

Yet those seven monks were not martyrs of their faith in the strictest sense. They were martyrs of love. They did not die because they were Christians. They died because they would not desert their Muslim friends, who depended on them and who lived in equal danger.

John Kiser is an international business executive and writer for the *Harvard Business Review* and the *Wall Street Journal*. In his book, *The Monks of Tibhirine: Faith, Love and Terror in Algeria*, he writes about the leader of their monastery, Christian de Cherge. As a young soldier in Algeria during the War of Independence, Christian had found the Muslims to be a people devoted to prayer and serving God. His monastery sought to expand traditional Christianity, to make a safe place for Islam, and to seek common ground, what he called "the notes that are in harmony."

On one occasion Christian took his guest, a Sufi Muslim and an old friend, on a tour of the monastery's chapel. Muslims typi-

cally find depictions of the crucifixion scandalous and deeply dis-
respectful of Jesus, whom they revere as one of God's great prophets, but the Islamic visitor was deeply moved by the large crucifix
in the monastery. Christian asked him: "When you look at the
cross, you see an image of Jesus—but how many crosses do you
see?"

"Perhaps three, certainly two," the Sufi replied, thinking a bit.
"There is one in front and one behind."

"Which comes from God?" asked Christian.

"The one in front," he said.

"Which comes from men?"

"The one behind."

"Which came first?"

"The one in front . . . God had to create the first before man
could make the second one."

"What is the meaning of the cross in front, of the man with his
arms extended?"

"When I extend my arms," his Muslim friend said, "it's for
embracing, for loving."

"And the other?"

"The other cross is an instrument of hatred, for disfiguring
love," said his friend.

"And this third cross, the cross between the crosses," they
wondered aloud, "isn't it perhaps the two of us in this common
effort we are making to loosen ourselves from the cross of evil and
sin behind, so we can bind ourselves to the cross of love in front?
[Isn't the struggle of moving from war to peace], from hatred to
love, a third cross?"

Christian alluded to the verses in the Koran that speak of the
death of Jesus. He interpreted them in his own particular way:
"They did not kill him for certain. God lifted him up to Him. God
is mighty and wise. Yes, by his death, [Jesus'] life was not taken. It
was transformed," said Christian. "It was love, not nails, which
attached him to the cross we carved for him. And it is love which
draws us to Him when he pardons His executioners."[81]

Three years later, at noon on May 23, Christian and the six other monks of Tibhirine, who had been kidnapped 56 days earlier, were found dead—an act of indescribable violence by a hate group of religious and political fundamentalists.

The following Sunday 40,000 churches throughout France tolled their bells for the monks. A memorial service was held the same day at Notre Dame Cathedral in Paris, where the seven candles that had been snuffed out three days earlier were relighted. "These candles represented the hope that the seven monks remained alive," said the Archbishop. "Let us now pray for those innocents who have been massacred and for all those whom the monks did not want to abandon . . . . Their death must be a sign of hope, that love is stronger than hatred."

Two days later, 10,000 people gathered opposite the Eiffel Tower to express solidarity with the Algerian people, and to condemn the barbarism. They came in silence, each person holding a white flower—a daisy, a rose, a carnation—accompanied by the doleful strains of Mahler's Fourth Symphony . . . . On each wall facing the plaza, a banner was hung bearing the an inscription by Christian de Cherge: "If we are silent, the stones themselves will cry out."

The next day, Christian's Last Will and Testament was published in the newspapers:

"My life is not worth more than any other—not less, not more," he writes. "Nor am I an innocent child. I have lived long enough to know that I, too, am an accomplice of the evil that seems to prevail in the world around, even that which might lash out blindly at me . . . .

"I know the contempt some people have for Algerians as a whole. I also know the caricatures of Islam that a certain (Islamic) ideology promotes. It is too easy for such people to dismiss, in good conscience, this religion as something hateful by associating it with violent extremists . . . .

"Obviously, my death will justify the opinion of all those who dismissed me as naïve or idealistic: 'Let him tell us what he thinks now.' But such people should know my death will satisfy my most burning curiosity. At last I will be able—if God pleases—to see the children of Islam as He sees them, illuminated in the glory of Christ, sharing in the gift of God's Passion and of the Spirit, whose secret joy will always be to bring forth our common humanity amidst our differences."

And then in what might almost be called a moment of clairvoyance, he writes to his assassin in language that recalls Jesus' final words on the cross:

"And to you, too, my friend of the last moment, who will not know what you are doing. Yes, for you, too, I wish this thank-you, this 'A-Dieu,' whose image is in you also, that we may meet in heaven, like happy thieves, if it pleases God, our common Father. Amen! Insha Allah!"[82]

Thousands of Algerian Muslims responded to the death of the monks with letters of regret, shame, and apology. A professor at the University of Algiers predicted shortly after the death of the monks: "One day, those seven monks will be considered saints by Muslims, Christians, and Jews."

Could it be that Christian's Muslim brother had it right that afternoon in the monastery? Could it be that there are actually three crosses in the crucifix?

"We are moved by the first cross, the cross that is Jesus himself embracing our own sorrows and brokenness in the love of God;

"We stand censured by the second cross, the cross we construct—the crosses of hatred and selfishness [of doctrinal and tribal exclusion] on which we crucify one another.

"But we are called to embrace the spirit of the humble and compassionate Christ to take up the third cross: the work of dismantling and leaving behind the crosses we have made in order to be transformed by the love of God made real for us in the cross of Christ."[83]

When Christian first met with the Muslim Sufis years before, one of them said, "We feel called by God to do something together with you. But we are not interested in theology. Theology rais-

es barriers between people. Let God invent something new between us. Love is what brings people together. And without bonds,
there can be no peace."[84]

My friends, the world is too small for our religious wars. As
George Bernard Shaw wrote in Anthony and Cleopatra: "Murder
shall breed murder, always in the name of right and honor and
peace, until at last the gods tire of blood and create a race that can
understand."

Now, more than any time in human history, we need to link
arms with one another, not use them against one another. May
that Muslim's prayer be ours as well:

"LET GOD INVENT SOMETHING NEW BETWEEN US."

A WORLD
BEYOND WAR

CHAPTER 17

KILLING FOR GOD

"It was, as the seasoned sailors call it,
the Perfect Storm."

Those of you who are parents can relate to the mother who ran into her son Jack's bedroom when she heard him scream and found his two-year-old sister pulling his hair. She gently released the little girl's grip and said comfortingly to Jack, "There, there. She didn't mean it. She just doesn't know that it hurts when someone pulls on your hair."

Mom was barely out of the room when this time it was the little girl who screamed. Rushing back in, she said, "What happened?"

"She knows now!" Jack explained.

Abe Lemmons, former Longhorn's basketball coach, was asked if he was bitter at Texas Athletic Director Deloss Dodds, who had fired him. He replied, "Not at all . . . but I plan to buy a glass-bottomed car so I can watch the look on his face when I run over him!"

A protestor with a Bible waves a placard outside a medical clinic: "For God's Sake, Kill the Baby-Killers!"

What is it within us that resonates with the slogan, "Don't get mad, just get even!"? Revenge is seldom the final answer but often the first defense. And, as Pascal said, "People never do evil so cheerfully as when they do it from religious conviction."

In 312 CE, Emperor Constantine saw a vision of the Christian Cross blazing before him as he went into battle. Written on the cross was, "By this sign thou shalt conquer."

In 1898, President William McKinley told new reporters how, after a sleepless night of dialogue with the Almighty, "God told me to take the Philippines."

In the mid-1960's, President Lyndon Johnson informed television audiences around the world that he had prayed for guidance in foreign policy and God had told him to send U.S. troops into Vietnam.

In the late 1990's, President George W. Bush as much as told the American people that he felt God had told him to send troops into Iraq.

In retaliation Saddam Hussein televised his speech to fellow

Iraqis to resist in the name of "God, the great Creator," and "hit back with capability and efficiency, relying on God the Almighty, at any hostile plane the aggressors fly to violate the airspace of your great country . . . . God is greatest and let the lowly people be humiliated."[85]

How in the Name of God, can we possibly stop the bloodshed that justifies itself "in the Name of God?"

In the Torah's telling of the Exodus story we have the beginnings of the Jewish Passover Festival, an unparalleled time of celebration of God's activity as Redeemer—an Old Testament "Easter," as some have called it. And yet, the redemption comes out of an experience of horrendous terror by the same God who kills innocent children for the sins of their parents. The darkness of the night matched the darkness of the deed. No household was spared; no barnyard escaped. It was sudden, infant death syndrome throughout Egypt that night. And throughout the night a cacophony of cries wailing from thousands of childless parents.

What kind of a God would kill innocent children? Even if they are the children of one's enemy. Doesn't God love Egyptians too?

It is significant that this was measure-for-measure retaliation for Pharaoh's effort to kill off all the male children of Israel. Because Pharaoh did not spare the firstborn of Yahweh, Yahweh did not spare the firstborn of Egypt, even Pharaoh's eldest son. True, people in that day were accustomed to thinking of supernatural activity in even more warlike terms than we do today. Still, it doesn't resolve the problem of God as "the Avenging Angel," the bringer of death.

If we identify God as "the slayer of the wicked," or of their innocent children, it is an easy reach for a nation or a self-appointed group to put on God's mantle of war and do God's work for God. And there are thousands of willing commandos out there ready to purify American society. What begins as a religious conviction to stop abortions by killing the doctors who perform them soon escalates into killing anyone who disagrees with us.

So, how do we stop the violence? The first step is to realize that

God is not on our side only. The second is to stop demonizing
those with whom we disagree or whom we do not understand. The
third step is to realize that we do not "have" all the truth and that
our stories may not be the last word. God alone is true. Not our
ideas about God.

There is an organization in California called "Citizens for
Excellence in Education," dedicated to restoring prayer to the public schools and the creationist version of Genesis to the class-
rooms. According to the *Wall Street Journal*, the group works to
elect Christian governmental officials, believing that government
should be "the police department within the Kingdom of God on
earth," ready to "impose God's vengeance upon those who abandon God's laws of justice."[87]

This is not the best of Christianity—nor is it excellence in education. This is a "theology of force and violence" which seeks to
destroy the other, not redeem them. The same thing happens
when any of us dehumanize or demonize another person or group
as a scapegoat for our own sins. We heap our own evil on them (as
they did to the innocent the Old Testament lambs) so that we can
feel justified in sending them away as outcasts, or worse, killing
them. We are performing this ritual slaughter day after day with
"those not like us":
- abortion doctors
- convicted felons
- immigrants
- gays and lesbians
- the unemployed
- welfare recipients and their hungry children
- liberals (and even conservatives)
- the federal government
- African American
- Whites
- Jews
- Hispanics
- Muslims

- the mentally ill,
- the poor of the earth . . . and so many others.

The symbol of redemption cannot be a slaughtered child—for the ancient Hebrews or for America. The blood on the doorpost was not a sign to God to change God's mind. It was a sign to the Israelites of God's faithfulness and promised redemption.

Three thousand years later, we need a better theology than the ancient Hebrew and classical Christian atonement theories of blood for blood. Jesus didn't die to change God's mind about our punishment. Jesus died because we couldn't make up our own mind to live with pure love and justice—so we killed it.

The point of it all is not there is something noble about shedding blood, or that murder atones for murder—an eye for an eye, a life for a life. The point is that one life is laid down willingly for another. It is not the sacrificial death that appeases an angry god. It is the heroic life lived for others that changes the world. What we Christians celebrate in the Sacrament of Holy Communion is Jesus' self-giving love completely poured out for us—and act of God's loving us to death, and beyond.

The only rationale for the Jews' continual remembrance of the Passover and the Christians' remembrance of the Death of Christ is to make sure that we do not allow it to happen again to anyone.

This is where the "debt of love," as Paul calls it, comes in. "Owe no one anything, except to love one another . . . . Love does no wrong to neighbor; therefore, love is the fulfilling of the law."[88]

If, "in the Name of God" we have destroyed our neighbor, then "in the Name of God" we can save our neighbors . . . and ourselves. There are a million ways to do that. Take welfare, for instance. We have made welfare into a sacrificial lamb; we have demonized the poor and the unemployed people who are receiving it. Most people on welfare—and I know a number of them—tell me they would much rather work for a living, put in an honest day's labor for an honest day's pay, and regain their self-respect. Why can't we respond to former President Clinton's challenge to hire somebody off welfare? If each faith community would take just one individual's welfare check, add a little money to make it a living wage, train them for a job in one of the congregant's companies, bring their children into our families, give them a hand in tutoring, as well as an extended home and family, it would empower them and enrich us. Granted, churches cannot solve the problems, but if every faith community in America hired one person off welfare, we would set an example for businesses and towns and nonprofit organizations to follow.

Let us resolve to banish the avenging angel and the death blows of poverty from the earth. Hungry children die one by one. They can be saved one by one.

Take any of the groups of people I just mentioned and think about it. In the Name of God, how can we more actively work for their good? To love anyone is to have faith and hope in them always. From the moment at which we begin to judge them, to limit our confidence in them, from that moment at which we label them, we reduce them to that label and cease to see them as our neighbor, our sister, and our brother.

We must dare to love in a world that has forgotten how.

> *"Love is filling from one's own,*
> *Another's cup.*
> *Love is the daily laying down*
> *And taking up;*
> *A choosing of the stony path*
> *Through each new day,*
> *That other feet may tread with ease*
> *A smother way.*
> *Love is not blind, but looks abroad*
> *Through other's eyes;*
> *And asks not, 'Must I give?'*
> *But 'May I sacrifice?'*
> *Love hides its grief, that other hearts*
> *And lip may sing;*

And burdened walks, that other lives
May buoyant wing.
Hast thou a love like this
Within thy soul?
'Twill crown thy life with bliss
when thou dost reach the goal."

In the Name of God, let us love one another!

CHAPTER 18

ONCE TO EVERY MAN AND NATION

*"Nobody cares about the storms
you've weathered.
Did you bring the ship in?"*

In December of 1844, a Harvard poet began protesting the upcoming U.S. war with Mexico. America had illegally annexed the territory of Texas. The action was violently opposed by the North because it contributed to the expansion of slavery and arguably fueled the beginnings of the Civil War.

A minister's son and grandson of a member of the Second Continental Congress, James Russell Lowell wrote the first ever poem to stop an international crime and repudiate a great social wrong. It is a clarion call for courageous fidelity to principle, and the earliest American example of the Social Gospel in a hymn.

> *"Once to Every Man and Nation*
> *Comes the moment to decide,*
> *In the strife of truth with falsehood,*
> *For the good or evil side;*
> *Some great cause, some new decision,*
> *Offering each the bloom or blight,*
> *And the choice goes by forever*
> *'Twixt the darkness and that light . . .*
> *Though the cause of evil prosper,*
> *Yet 'tis truth alone is strong;*
> *Though her cause bring fame and profit,*
> *And upon the throne be wrong,*
> *Yet that scaffold sways the future,*
> *And behind the dim unknown,*
> *Standeth God within the shadow*
> *Keeping watch above His own."*[89]

Millions of voices around the world have been raised against, and some in support of, our present war in Iraq.

- Each voice has its own passion and justification.
- Each voice ultimately seeks the same goal:
  peace on earth and goodwill to humanity.
- Each voice claims to *"side with truth."*

- Each voice believes that, *"Though the cause of evil prosper, yet 'tis truth alone is strong."*
- Each voice knows that, *"Truth is ever on the scaffold, wrong is ever on the throne."*

And many of these voices believe that, *"Beyond the dim unknown standeth God within the shadow, keeping watch above His own."*

With the scaffold of truth swaying over us, the question for each of us this Day of Decision is, "What now?"

The juxtaposition of peace and war has never felt so visceral to me. Time and again, I find myself, like you, asking where I might go to gain some perspective on these wrenching questions of war and peace.

Instinctively for Christians, the first place to turn is the Bible. But the fact is the BIBLE IS AMBIVALENT ON THE THEME OF WAR. Age after age, peacemakers have repeated the grand Biblical injunctions inscribed on the Isaiah Wall opposite the United Nations: "And they shall beat their swords into ploughshares, their spears into pruning hooks; nation shall not lift up sword against nation, neither shall they learn war anymore."[90]

Yet the third chapter of Joel proclaims a time to "beat ploughshares into swords, pruning hooks into spears; let the weak say, 'I am a warrior.'"[91] Two diametrically opposed commands for different people at different times from the same Bible.

Certainly, you say, the Christian Religion has the answer. But, THE CHURCH HAS BEEN NO LESS AMBIVALENT THAN THE BIBLE REGARDING WAR. You can pretty much classify the church's changing attitudes toward war into four categories: *pacifism*, the *"just war,"* the *"crusade,"* and *"Christian realism."*

From the time of those first Jewish followers of Jesus, most of the early Christians took a *pacifist* position against all war, following the example of Jesus. For the first several hundred years, military service in the Roman army was grounds for excommunication from the church.

When Emperor Constantine made Christianity the "most

favored religion" in the 4th century, the tables turned. Christian resistance to military service was met with imprisonment or death. So the church borrowed the concept of the *"just war"* from Classical thought, and reframed it as a Christian doctrine.

During the Middle Ages, the *religious crusade* became the ideal. This was a holy war (a "jihad," if you will), fought under the auspices of the church, not on behalf of *justice* of life and property, but on behalf of an *ideology*, the Christian Religion, and a goal, Unbounded Power. Once the enemy was demonized as "the evil empire," all "just war" codes and criteria broke down.

World War I was treated as a *crusade* by many Christians. *Pacifism* was prevalent between the two World Wars. And the *"just war"* has been the norm with Catholics and most Protestants since World War II. In the 1950's, theologian Reinhold Niebuhr coined what he called *"Christian Realism."* That is to say, we live in a fallen world and must do the best we can. Moral choice is rarely between the moral and the immoral; it is between the immoral and the less moral.

So, it is clear that not only the Bible, but 2,000 years of Christian history and theology are ambivalent on the issues of war. Actually, everybody is ambivalent. Albert Camus talked of going into war "with weapons in our hands and a lump in our throats."

Having said all this, I agree 100% with Bill Coffin when he said: "About the use of force I think we *should* be ambivalent—the dilemmas are real. All we can say for sure is that while force may be *necessary*, what is wrong—always wrong—is *the desire to use it.*"[92] "The warhorse is a vain hope for victory," said the Psalmist. "And by its great might it cannot save."

We all may be ambivalent about our use of force. We may even disagree on the morality of first-strike, preemptive war. But when it comes to the use of nuclear weapons, there should not be a Christian alive who would not say "amen" to the words of Monsignor Bruce Kent: "We did not make the planet; we do not own the planet; and we have no right to wreck the planet."

As Jimmy Carter said when he accepted the Nobel Peace Prize,

"War may sometimes be a necessary evil, but no matter how necessary, it is always an evil, never a good."

Sincere, well-meaning people disagree. Dissent is not disloyal . . . subservience is. That is the reality of the human condition and the strength of a democracy. In a time of war, we may feel tempted to silence those who voice dissent, as though it were unpatriotic. Never do that! America was born out of protest. Every freedom we hold dear in this nation was initially a courageous act of individual conscience. We are in this fight to bring freedom of speech to Iraq, not to smother it back home.

There are a number of ambiguities surrounding this present war. But some things are clear and unambiguous. Let us covenant together to be of one voice and one heart on these essentials:

FIRST: LET US NOT FORSAKE OUR COURAGEOUS SOLDIERS, who were not conscripted, as most warriors are, but voluntarily chose to put their lives on the line for us. I come from a strong stock of Scottish Camerons and American Cherokee, no strangers to the violence of war. My great-great-grandfather fought for the North in the Civil War. My grandfather fought "The Battle to End All Wars" in the First World War. My grandmother served in the Women's Ambulance Corp. My father served in the Pacific Theatre in World War II. My father-in-law was an Allied radio and signal operator in England and France. My brother-in-law served with honors near the front lines in the first Gulf War. My mother served her country as a civilian informant, a kind of secret agent within Communist cell groups during the Cold War. The only reason I was not drafted in the 1960's was because I was enrolled in Divinity School. The government thought my religious colleagues and I would be more helpful at home in buoying-up the spirits of those who were left behind.

War has been the backdrop of my life as long as I can remember. Hate war as I do, I will be forever grateful to those who have served their country in the military on my behalf. I would not for a moment cast aspersions on their motives for fighting, their Christian convictions, nor their quest for peace at the end. We owe our men and women in the armed services nothing short of our very lives. They followed their heart, not just their papers. They put themselves in harm's way for me and my family, for each of you, and for millions of others. They are, tragically, the unsung heroes of our precious freedoms. Let us never forget that they were willing to, and many did, lay down their lives for us, that we might lay down our lives for others. Let us not repeat the mistakes of Vietnam. Our daily prayers must be that our men and women in uniform accomplish their mission of peacekeeping in Iraq honorably, quickly, humbly, with honor, and return home to us proudly—alive, whole, and soon.

SECOND: LET US NOT GLORIFY WAR. War is so energizing, so passionate, and so life-giving. Even with its carnage it offers us what we long for in life, the allusion of heroism. It can give us purpose, meaning, a reason for living. War is an enticing elixir from our trivial pursuits.

War brings out the best as well as the worst of us: our loyalty, our courage, our venturesomeness, our care for the downtrodden, our capacity for self-sacrifice. "It is fortunate that war is hell," said General William Sherman, "or men would love it too much."

But let us also remember, as General George Washington put it: "As necessary as war might be, it is a 'plague to mankind.'"

And as General Dwight D. Eisenhower declared:

Every gun that is made,
Every warship launched,
Every rocket fired signifies,
In the final sense,
A theft from those who hunger and are not fed,
Those who are cold and are not clothed.

This world in arms is not spending money alone.
It is spending the sweat of its laborers,
The genius of its scientists,
The hopes of its children . . . .
I hate war!"

"It is the business of the churches," declared Military Field-Marshal Earl Haig, "to make my business impossible." So let us fulfill that calling in our time.

THIRD: LET US PRAY FOR OUR ENEMIES. This is not a suggestion from Jesus; it is a command. "Every man's death diminishes me," wrote John Donne, "for I am a part of the whole."

Every visual image we see on TV of havoc wrought by yet another devastating cruise missile or suicide bomber must become for us a call to prayer. Every air raid siren and sound of explosion should be for us a call to confession and pardon. At the least, when we see and hear this cacophony of pain over and over on every feed of the news monitor, we can whisper a prayer for the wife and the child, the sister and the brother, the parents and the lover, of that valiant warrior who just died, regardless of whose side they were on: *"Lord have mercy, Christ have mercy, Lord have mercy."*

I am so encouraged every time I remember the CNN coverage of that Marine chaplain admonishing his platoon with the directive: "Pray not only for yourself, but for your enemies as well. After all, they are just soldiers, like you, doing what they are ordered to do." God bless those kinds of military chaplains. When we pray for the nameless and faceless enemy, we give him or her a name and a face: "Child of God," "Face of Jesus," "Brother and Sister in our shared humanity."

FOURTH: LET US NOT BE DRIVEN BY FEAR. Thomas Merton put it well: "Where there is no love of man, no love of life, then make all the laws you want, all the edicts and treaties—as long as you see your fellow man as a being essentially to be feared, mistrusted, hated and destroyed, there cannot be peace on earth."

Let us remember that war is a cowardly escape from the giant problems of peace. We must not live our lives in fear of the unknown. Fear is the enemy of learning; it gives ignorance its power. Rather, let us recommit ourselves to a new coalition of moral strength, not just of those who would follow us in military ventures, but those who would work together with us in building a new world for a new day. Let us not be heady with arrogant pride or national bullying and opportunism. Let us recommit ourselves to standing strong in partnership with our allies around the world. Let us not dissert, but rather put more spine into the United Nations, NATO, the European Union, and every alliance that works for the greater good, not only of its own nation, but of the Commonwealth of Nations.

FINALLY: LET US LEAVE A LEGACY FOR OUR FIGHTING SONS AND DAUGHTERS that when they return, they will find a new America, a more moral America, a more decent America. Let them find on these shores which they have protected from afar a new compassion for
- war veterans without jobs, family, and sanity,
- children without meals or education,
- youth without purpose or hope,
- elderly without medical care,
- left-out ones without voice,
- immigrants without representation,
- poor without advocacy,
- teachers without textbooks,
- Muslims without safety, and
- disenfranchised without voice.

When the narrow sympathies of some and the fear of others combine to mute this generous cry, may we give it new voice in our day.

Let those patriots who are at this moment so bravely fighting alongside those who are dying for America and the free world, find realized when they return to us the dream of our first Pilgrims on the Arbella, anchored off the New England coast: that we have, in their absence, become as John Winthrop proclaimed, *"a city upon a hill; the eyes of all people . . . upon us . . . that we delight in each other, make other's conditions our own, rejoice together, mourn together, labor and suffer together, always having before our eyes our community as members of the same body."*

When they return to the shores of their homeland, may they

join us, as Abraham Lincoln predicted, to *"strive on to finish the work we are in, to bind up the nation's wounds, to care for [the one] who shall have borne the battle, and for his widow and his orphan—to do all which may achieve and cherish a just and lasting peace among ourselves and with all nations."*

And with Lincoln, may we today keep alive *"the mystic chord of memory, stretched from every battlefield and patriot grave to every living heart and hearthstone all over this broad land, [which] will yet swell the chorus of the Union, when again touched, as surely they will be, by the better angels of our nature."*[94]

"Once to Every Man and Nation Comes a Moment to Decide"![95] This is America's defining moment. "God give us Wisdom, God give us Courage, For the living of these days."[96]

> *"Our father's God to thee*
> *Author of liberty*
> *To thee we sing.*
> *Long may our land be bright*
> *With freedom's holy light*
> *Protect us by Thy might*
> *Great God, our king.*[97]

CHAPTER 19

A TRIBUTE TO WILLIAM SLOANE COFFIN IN HIS OWN WORDS

Compiled and Preached
by The Reverend Dr. Gary A. Wilburn
EASTER SUNDAY
April 16, 2006
[In Memoriam: William Sloan Coffin
June 1, 1924—April 12, 2006]

"To Bill with Great Love and Appreciation"

—GARY

Whand makes Easter so much fun is all the finery: the chickens, the rabbits, the lambs, the eggs, the forsythia, the cherry blossoms . . .and now, finally, the warm air—altogether a glorious day!

[A crowd like this one this Easter morning] reminds me of all the undergraduates I knew and loved, many now crowding sixty, even seventy. Some of them have aged like vintage wine, heeding Albert Camus's wisdom: "To grow old is to pass from passion to compassion."

A few of them, however, looking back on the springtime of their lives, say, "Ah, those were the days!"—and the worst of it is, they're right! It was not the days, I suspect, but they who used to be better!

You have to unlearn as well as learn, to clear away the weeds and thickets in order to see more clearly the various paths ahead. [The same applies to our faith.]

Harry Emerson Fosdick, the founding pastor of Riverside Church in New York, once wrote, "The world has tried in two ways to get rid of Jesus: first, by crucifying him, and second, by worshipping him." Jesus doesn't ask us to worship him. [In fact, he specifically told his followers not to worship him.] He said, "Follow me." Faith is a matter of being faithful. It's not believing without proof; it's trusting without reservation.

Over the years I have been convinced that the more important question is not who believes in God, but in whom does God believe? Rather than claim God for our side, it's better to wonder whether we are on God's side. Faith is being grasped by the power of love, and there are many atheists with "believing" hearts—the part of us that should be religious if you can offer only one.

God's love doesn't seek value; it creates it. It's not because we have value that we are loved. It is because we are loved that we have value. Our value is a gift, not an achievement. Just think: we never have to *prove ourselves*; that's already taken care of. All we have to do is to *express ourselves*–to return God's love with our own.

But [to return to this morning's theme], what makes Easter so exciting is the cosmic quality of it. For Easter has less to do with one person's escape from the grave than with the victory of seemingly powerless love over loveless power. Easter represents a *demand* as well as a *promise*, a demand not that we *sympathize* with the *crucified Christ*, but that we *pledge our loyalty* to the *risen one*. That means an end to all loyalties, to all people, and to all institutions that crucify.

For example, I don't see how we can proclaim allegiance to the Risen Lord and remain indifferent to our government's [and the world's] intention not to abolish nuclear weapons. Or how can we think that the Risen Lord would applaud an economic system that reverses the priorities of Mary's Magnificat - filling the rich with good things and sending the poor away empty? (Almost one American child in four lives below the poverty line, and one in three children of the world exist in terribly horrible poverty.)

Few of us are truly evil; the trouble is, most of us mean well–feebly. We are just not serious. We carry around justice, love, and peace in our shopping carts, but along with a lot of other things that make for injustice, hatred, and war. Churches in our day are a bit like families: they tend to be havens in a heartless world, but they reinforce that world by caring more for its victims than by challenging its assumptions.

Christ wants us to challenge the assumptions of our nation and world, just as he challenged those of his. In a democracy dissent is not disloyal. Christ today wants his disciples to tell the nations that their disastrous cult of power leads to the pretensions of the powerful, and to the despair of the powerless, leaving all lovers of life filled with unutterable sadness.

What I think God wants us to do is not practice *piecemeal charity* but engage in *wholesale justice*. Justice is at the heart of religious faith. When we see Christ empowering the poor, scorning the powerful, healing the world's hurts, we are seeing transparently the power of God at work.

God is not too hard to believe in. God is too good to believe in, we being such strangers to such goodness. Two things are clear to me: that almost every square inch of the earth's surface is soaked with the tears and blood of the innocent . . . and that it's not God's doing. It's our doing. That's human malpractice. Don't chalk it up to God. Every time people see the innocent suffering, and lift their eyes to heaven and say, "God, how could you let this happen?" it's well to remember that exactly at that moment God is asking exactly the same question of us: "How could you let this happen?"

If you back off from every little controversy in your life you're not alive . . . and what's more, you're boring! [The truth is] you can be more alive in pain than in complacency. It's not enough to pray, "Grant us peace in our time, O Lord." God must be saying, "Oh, come off it! What are you going to do for peace, for heaven's sake?" It's not enough to pray for peace. You have to work for justice. You have to suffer for it, and you have to endure a lot for it. So don't just pray about it.

People in high places make me really angry—the way that [some] corporations are now behaving, the way the United States government is behaving. What makes me angry is that they are so callous, really callous. When you see uncaring people in high places, everybody should be mad as hell.

Self-righteousness destroys our capacity for self-criticism. It makes it very hard to be humble, and it destroys the sense of oneness all human beings should have, one with another.

My understanding of Christianity is that it underlies all progressive moves to implement more justice, to get a higher degree of peace in the world. The impulse to love God and neighbor, that impulse is at the heart of Judaism, Islam, Christianity [and the other religions of the world]. God is not confined to Christians.

I am not a pacifist. About the use of force I think we should be ambivalent—the dilemmas are real. All we can say for sure is that while force may be necessary, what is wrong—always wrong—is the desire to use it. It is hard to get even with violent people [especially terrorists]. What is easy is to get more and more like them.

"The warhorse is a vain hope for victory, and by its great might it cannot save." (Psalm 33) War is a coward's escape from the problems of peace.

God is not mocked: what is grossly immoral cannot in the long run be politically expedient. "The earth is the Lord's and the fullness thereof." Only reverence can restrain violence, be it violence against nature or against each other.

President Bush rightly spoke of an "axis of evil," but it is not Iran, Iraq, and North Korea. A far more dangerous trio would be: environmental degradation, pandemic poverty, and a world awash with weapons. Far beyond individuals, communities, and nations, the world itself is on the brink of destruction. If we were serious, with the other nations, to engage the war on poverty around the world, that would stem the flow of recruits to the ranks of terrorists.

Every nation makes decisions based on self-interest and defends them on the basis of morality. In our time all it takes for evil to flourish is for a few good men to be a little wrong and have a great deal of power and for the vast majority of their fellow citizens to remain indifferent. The danger today is that we might become more concerned with defense than with [being a country] worth defending.

Terrorism is a clear and present danger, but our present policies are nourishing rather than restraining terrorists . . . . Let's not forget what that Israeli journalist wrote: "The terrorism of suicide bombers is born of despair. There is no military solution to despair."

Norman Mailer compared our present pursuit of terrorists to a Sherman tank going after a hornet hiding in a building. By the time the building is flattened, arousing considerable resentment, the hornet is safely in the attic next door. With terrorist cells in over sixty nations we need allies, lots of them, who think not ill but well of us. Most of all, we must agree to be governed by the force of law, not by the law of force.

For our presently tormented and endangered planet to survive, it will require a politically committed spirituality. Patriotism at the expense of another nation is as wicked as racism at the expense of another race. Let us resolve to be patriots always, nationalists never. Let us love our country, but

> *". . . pledge allegiance to the earth,*
> *and to the flora and fauna and human life that it supports;*
> *one planet indivisible, with clean air, soil and water;*
> *with liberty, justice and peace for all."*

Before I die, I want to see all nuclear missiles beaten into homes for the homeless and land for the landless, into day-care centers and good schools for our poorest kids and compassionate care for our elderly.

Only God has the right to destroy all life on the planet. We haven't the authority; we only have the power. Therefore, to threaten to use nuclear weapons must be an abomination in the sight of God. We have to recognize a single standard for all nuclear weapons: either universal permission or universal abolition.

Courage means being well aware of the worst that can happen, being scared almost to death and then doing the right thing anyhow. As Robert Kennedy said so well, "Only those who dare to fail greatly can ever achieve greatly."

[We] can either follow [our] fears or be led by [our] values and [our] passions. All of this fear-mongering today (of immigrants, homosexuals, crime, and terrorists), I'm afraid, is quite deliberate because the more you can make people fear, the more a government can control you. The American people don't feel a sense of personal accountability for what the nation should stand for. No one need be afraid of fear; only afraid that fear will stop him or her from doing what's right.

[Yet, in the face of all of this . . .] I remain *hopeful*. Hope needs to be understood as a reflection of the state of your soul, not as reflection of the circumstances that surround your days. Hope is not the equivalent of optimism. The opposite of hope is not pessimism, but despair. Hope is about keeping the faith despite the evidence so that the evidence has a chance of changing.

If Christ never allowed his soul to be cornered with despair—and his was maybe the greatest miscarriage of justice in the world—who the hell am I to say I'm going to despair a bit? Hope criticizes what is, hopelessness rationalizes it. Hope resists, hopelessness adapts. *Hope arouses, as nothing else can, a passion for the possible!*

There never was a night or a problem that could defeat sunrise or hope!

We may not know *what* is beyond the grave, but we do know *who* is beyond the grave. And there is more *mercy* in him than *sin* in us, more *faith* in him than *doubt* in us, and more *hope* for the world in him than in anything else on the horizon.

"Thine is the Glory, Risen, Conquering Son, Endless is the Victory, Thou o'er Death hast won."

William Sloane Coffin died four days before this sermon was preached. It is a composite of his own words in sermons, books, and interviews over the years. See "NOTES" for the sources that were the most helpful to me in this compilation—G.A.W.

EPILOGUE

(A LETTER FROM THE AUTHOR)
"LIVE LIKE YOU WERE DYING"

Joe Dimaggio, the greatest ballplayer ever, suffered through every game with a terribly painful bone spur. When asked why he played so hard every game, he answered, *"Because there might be someone out there who never saw me play before!"*

Before he retired, with a record 56 consecutive games of safe hits, "Joltin' Joe" had led the New York Yankees to ten American League championships and nine World Series titles.

"If there ever comes a time when the game isn't fun any longer," said Joe, *"I've played my last game of ball!"*

That is exactly how I feel. And the game is still fun!

I was recently diagnosed with a condition called "Lower Motor Neuron Disease" (a form of ALS). They call it "lower" because eventually it affects everything below the top of the spinal column. The neurons, the electrical impulses, cannot get through. Eventually the muscles atrophy for lack of fuel, as it were.

However, I am not looking at this as a terminal illness. First of all, because not all diagnoses are entirely accurate. Second, because I believe in prayer. I think that what we call "miracles" are really "nature unencumbered." I believe that God not only surrounds us, but is actually inside each of us—woven into the very fabric of our beings. God exists in our very own DNA—as well as in the DNA of the universe. God/nature is always spawning new life to spring forth, always developing new "connections" between our nerve fibers as well as between our bodies and our spirits and the universe: always reshaping things to fit together and connect as they were intended. So I'm practicing the art of "unencumbering" the natural health of my body by trying to live each day with love and hope, rather than fear and anxiety.

When my wife Bev and I first heard the doctor's diagnosis, we had a good long cry. Then we told our families and had another good cry. Then I remembered that great country-western song by Tim McGraw. It's about a cowboy who thought he'd live forever.

> *"He said: 'I was in my early forties,*
> *With a lot of life before me,*
> *An' a moment came that stopped me on a dime.*
> *I spent most of the next days,*
> *Looking at the x-rays,*
> *An' talkin' 'bout the options, an' talkin' 'bout sweet time."*
> *I asked him when it sank in,*
> *That this might really be the real end . . .*
> *"How's it hit you when you get that kind of news?*
> *Man, whatcha do?"*

> *An' he said: "I went sky diving, I went rocky mountain climbing,*
> *I went two-point-seven seconds on a bull named Fu Man Chu.*
> *And I loved deeper, and I spoke sweeter,*
> *And I gave forgiveness I'd been denying."*
> *An' he said: "Some day, I hope you get the chance,*
> *to live like you were dyin'."*[98]

I have thought about that song every day since we heard the news. I find myself singing it under my breath. Because, someday, we are all going to die. Yet even though we all know it, most of us spend our lives denying it . . . pretending as if we will live forever. You can't blame us . . . who wants to deal with their eventual demise?

As Francis Bacon once said, "Men fear death . . . as children fear to go into the dark."

But, you know what? At this stage at least, I do not fear the unknown of death. As a Christian, I know deep in my gut that I *came from God*, and that at some time in the future, *I am returning to God. "Whom on earth have we but Thee, dear God . . .whom in heaven beside Thee, o Lord? Thou art the Alpha and the Omega, the Beginning and the End . . . the beginning of our journeys, and our journeys' end."*

So I am in no way concerned about my eternal destination. My faith has taught me that my life will not disintegrate into nothingness, but that at some point I will rejoin the company of all who have gone before, and all who are to come. I believe all of us will meet again. It is together with this eternal "company of the beloved" that we will be united—where our lives and loves will go on in that New World where you and I will continue to discover our true selves.

Eternity is not an issue. The issue is *today*.

Many of us have read the moving little book, *Tuesdays with Morrie*. It is the story of Morrie Schwartz, a college professor, who was diagnosed with amyotrophic lateral sclerosis (ALS), also known as "Lou Gehrig's Disease." Morrie began to deal with his own imminent death in a realistic, powerful, and courageous way. He invited a former student, Mitch Albom, to sit and talk with him each week. Knowing that his friend was dying, Mitch visited with Morrie in his study every Tuesday, week after week, month after month, just as they used to back in college.

"Do I wither up and disappear?" Morrie conjectured one morning, *"or do I make the most out of my time left?"* Of course, he chose to make the most of his time. He told his friends that if they really wanted to help him, they would treat him not with sympathy but with visits, phone calls, a sharing of their problems . . . the way they had always shared their problems . . . because Morrie had been a wonderful listener . . . . He was intent on proving that dying was not synonymous with uselessness . . . .

"Am I going to withdraw from the world, like most people do—or am I going to live?," Morrie asked himself. *"I decided I'm going to live, or at least try to live, the way I want, with dignity, with courage, with*

humor, with composure.[99]

As Tim McGraw puts it in the mouth of that country cowboy who had just been told of his prognosis:

> *"He said, 'I was finally the husband,*
> *That most of the time I wasn't.*
> *An' I became a friend a friend would like to have.*
> *And all of a sudden goin' fishin',*
> *Wasn't such an imposition,*
> *And I went three times that year I lost my Dad.*
> *Well, I finally read the Good Book,*
> *And I took a good long hard look,*
> *At what I'd do if I could do it all again . . ."*[100]

As I think more about it these days, life is at best unpredictable. None of us know how we will live or long we will live. When you think about it, we all have a "fatal disease"—We call it LIFE!

Death is good because it puts a limit on the number of days we have to accomplish our goals. If we were given an infinite amount of time in this world, most of us would never be driven to attain anything. We would always feel that we have so much more time to complete our tasks. Knowing that our days are numbered, we are motivated to strive for greatness. That's why Joe Dimaggio played so hard. Because there might be someone in the stands that night who never before saw him play.

Life begins again with every breath—and with every sunrise. Our Jewish friends have a time-honored custom of reciting the same prayer every morning upon awakening:

> *"I thank You, Living and Enduring King,*
> *for You have returned my soul to me, great is Your faithfulness!"*[101]

Maybe, in order to get the most out of it, we should all try to live every day as if we were dying . . . because the truth is, we are! When Lou Gehrig announced to his fans in Yankee Stadium that he had contracted the disease that was destined to be named after him, he said, *"Today I consider myself the luckiest man on the face of the earth. I might have had a tough break, but I have an awful lot to live for."*

"Again, the question to ask is *not 'Why?'* . . . 'Why did this happen? Why me? Why now? . . . W*hy?*' gets us nowhere. The only question worth asking is '*Where?'* . . . 'Where do we go from here?'

"And part of that answer must be 'together.' Together we kneel. Together we walk, holding one another's hands, holding one another up. As for a life that ends too soon, in the eye of eternity the only lives that end too soon are those that won't live on in others' hearts."[102] And have no fear, ours will live on.

So what finally happens to that country cowboy who was *"stopped on a dime"* by his x-rays? The same thing that happens to you and me when we look death straight in the eye, and look right through it. And then end up sayin'...

> *"Some day, I hope you get the chance,*
> *To live like you were dyin'.*
> *Like tomorrow was a gift.*
> *And you got eternity,*
> *To think about what you'd do with it.*
> *An' what did you do with it?*
> *An' what can I do with it?*
> *An' what would I do with it?"*

You know one of the things we can do with it? Just what he did.

> *"[I went] sky diving, I went rocky mountain climbing,*
> *I went two-point-seven seconds on a bull named Fu Man Chu.*
> *And then I loved deeper and I spoke sweeter,*
> *And I gave forgiveness I'd been denying.*
> *An' he said: "Some day, I hope you get the chance,*
> *To live like you were dyin'."*[103]

Thanks be to God.

NOTES

PREFACE

1. Marty Kaplan, *The New York Times*, March 31, 1997.
2. James Turner, *Without God, Without Creed: The Origins of Unbelief in America*, (Baltimore: The Johns Hopkins University Press, 1985), p. XI.
3. I Timothy 4:10.
4. I am most grateful for the work of The Reverend James Adams, Founder & Former President of *The Center for Progressive Christianity*, Cambridge, MA (President's Report, May 1998, pp. 1-4), as well as to The Reverend Fred Plumer, the new President of TCPC, and our many affiliates (www//tcpc.org).
5. William Sloane Coffin, *The Heart is a Little to the Left: Essays on Public Morality*

POSITIONING OUR SAILS TO THE WIND

6. Quite possibly a mythical tale, "The Legend of Eleazar Hull" appears in William Muehl's, "God Has No Pride," *All the Damned Angels* (Philadelphia: Pilgrim Press, 1972), p. 15.
7. William Sloane Coffin, Jr., *Credo* (Louisville, Kentucky: Westminster John Knox, 2003).
8. Ibid.

LEAVING OUR OUTGROWN SHELLS

9. Thomas Howard, *Christ the Tiger: A Postscript to Dogma* (Philadelphia: J.B. Lippincott Company, 1967), pp. 7-8.
10. Tom Stella, *A Faith Worth Believing: Finding New Life Beyond the Rules of Religion* (San Francisco: HarperSanFrancisco, 2004), pp. 13-15.
11. Howard, op. cit., p. 82.

DRAGON TERRITORIES

12. Bill Moyers, "9/11 and The Sport of God," an address to Union Theological Seminary, New York City, September 7, 2005.
13. "The Eight Points of Progressive Christianity," 2003 version, The Center for Progressive Christianity, tcpc.org.
14. "The Navy Hymn," William Whiting, 1860.

THE ABSENCE OF GOD

15. Associated Press/Ipsos Public Affairs, reported in *Christian Century*, June

28, 2005, p. 9.

16. William Sloane Coffin, *Letters to a Young Doubter* (Louisville: Westminster John Knox Press, 2005), p. 18.

17. Karen Armstrong, *A History of God* (New York: Ballantine Books, 1993).

18. Karl Barth, cited by Robert P. Carroll, *The Bible as a Problem for Christianity* (Philadelphia: Trinity Press International, 1991).

19. Anthony Bloom, *Beginning to Pray* (New York: Paulist Press, 1970), p. 17.

20. William H. Willimon, "To See God," *Pulpit Resource*, October 20, 1996, p. 13.

21. William Sloane Coffin, *Credo* (Louisville: Westminster John Knox Press, 2004), p. 124.

22. William Sloane Coffin, *Letters*, op. cit., pp. 24, 25.

ENTERING THE DEEP SEA OF MYSTERY

23. Nikos Kazantzakis, *Zorba the Greek*, (New York: Simon and Schuster, 1952), p. 51.

24. John Shelby Spong, "Pre-Modern Theology in Public Life," August 3, 2005, "A New Christianity for a New World," www.support@johnshelbspong.com.

FATHER GOD OR MOTHER NATURE?

25. William Shakespeare, "As You Like It," Act 2, Scene 1.

26. Tom Stella, *A Faith Worth Believing: Finding New Life Beyond the Rules of Religion* (San Francisco: HarperSanFrancisco, 2004), pp. 27-28.

27. Philip Clayton, "Emerging God: Theology for a Complex Universe," *Christian Century*, January 13, 2004, p. 3.

28. Marcus J. Borg, *The Heart of Christianity: Rediscovering a Life of Faith* (San Francisco: HarperSanFrancisco, 1995), p. 67.

29. Acts 15: 22-29.

30. John Zuck, "Biblical Panentheism" *http://www.frimmin.com/faith/godinall.html.)*

31. Ibid.

32. Philip Clayton, cited by Martin Marty, "Context," April 2004, Part A, pp. 4, 5.

33. "Morning Has Broken," Eleanor Farjeon, 1931.

DEAD IN THE WATER?

34. Philip Newell, *Listening for the Heartbeat of God* (London: SPCK, 1997), p. 3.

35. Ibid., p. 4.

36. Gerard Manley Hopkins, in Gardner & Mackenzie (editors), *The Poems of Gerard Manley Hopkins* (Oxford: Oxford University Press, 1967), p. 66.

37. George F. MacLeod, *The Whole Earth Shall Cry Glory* (Scotland: Wild Goose Publications, The Iona Community, 1985), p. 16.

DISCOVERING THE PRIMEVAL POOL
38. Ben Campbell Johnson, *To Pray God's Will: Continuing the Journey* (Philadelphia: The Westminster Press, 1987), pp.11-12.
39. Ian Fisher, "Cease-Fire in Macedonia Stops the Guns But Not the Ethnic Distrust and Bitterness," *New York Times International*, Saturday, July 7, 2001, p. A3.
40. Coleridge, "Rime of the Ancient Mariner," Part 7, Stanza 23.

A FINGER POINTING TO THE MOON
41. Robert Farrar Capon, *Hunting the Divine Fox* (New York: Seabury Press, 1974), p. 90.
42. Paul Alan Laughlin, *Remedial Christianity*, op cit., p.75
43. Marcus Borg, *The Heart of Christianity*, op cit., p. 81.
44. Paul Laughlin, op. cit.
45. Walter Wink, cited by Alan Jones, p. 2.
46. Fred Plumer, "The Eight Points of Progressive Christianity," TCPC, op. cit.

THE CELTIC SECRET
47. Verna Todd, "Celtic Spirituality: A World Alive With God's Presence," *Hungryhearts News*, the Spiritual Formation Program of the Presbyterian Church (U.S.A.), Louisville, KY, Summer, 1999, p. 3.
48. Ibid.
49. Matthew Fox, *Original Blessing: A Primer in Creation Spirituality* (New Mexico: Bear & Company, 1983), p. 46.
50. Elie Wiesel, *Messengers of God* (New York: 1976), p. 29.
51. Matthew Fox, op. cit., p. 48.
52. Ibid.
53. William Eckhardt, *Compassion: Toward a Science of Value* (Oakville, Ontario: 1973), pp. 4f.
54. Verna Todd, op. cit., p. 4.
55. From the *Carmina Gadelica*, a collection of Gaelic blessings and prayers gathered and translated by Alexander Carmichael; first volumes published in 1899.

THE MEANING OF JESUS' LIFE AND DEATH
56. Laughlin, *Remedial Christianity*, op. cit., p. 1.
57. Borg, *The Heart of Christianity*, op. cit., p. 91.
58. Spong, *A New Christianity for a New World*, op. cit., p. 127.

SACRIFICIAL LAMB OR ENEMY OF THE STATE?
59. Mark Juergensmeyer, *Terror in the Mind of God: The Global Rise of Religious Violence* (Berkeley: University of California Press, 2000), p. 216.
60. Ibid., p. 20.

61. Ibid., pp. xi, xii.
62. Raymond Schwager, cited by Walter Wink, *The Powers That Be: Theology for a New Millennium* (New York: Galilee Doubleday, 1998), pp. 84-85.
63. Walter Brueggemann, *The Prophetic Imagination* (Philadelphia: Fortress Press, 1978), chapter 1.
64. Jurgen Moltmann, Nicholas Wolterstorff, Ellen T. Cherry, *A Passion for God's Reign: Theology, Christian Learning, and the Christian Self* (Grand Rapids: Eerdmans, 1998), p. 2.
65. John Shelby Spong, *A New Christianity for a New World: Why Traditional Faith Is Dying & How a New Faith Is Being Born* (San Francisco: HarperSanFrancisco, 2001), p.125.

ONE LESS ROCKET SCIENTIST...
ONE MORE WHALE RIDER

66. Jay Cormier, "Connections" (MediaWorks, Londonderry, N.H.), October, 2004, p. 4.
67. Karen Armstrong, *The Spiral Staircase: My Climb Out of Darkness* (New York: Alfred A. Knoph, a division of Random House, 2004), pp. 270-271.
68. William Sloane Coffin, *A Passion for the Possible: A Message to U.S. Churches* (Louisville, KY: Westminster/John Knox Press, 1993), p. 82.

OUR GATEWAY INTO GOD'S REALM

69. Marcus Borg, *Reading the Bible Again for the First Time: Taking the Bible Seriously but Not Literally* (San Francisco: HarperSanFrancisco, 2001), pp. 216-217.
70. I John 4:10.
71. Borg, op. cit., p. 218.
72. Quoted from a *New York Times* op-ed piece by William Sloan Coffin, 2000.
73. Joseph C. Hough, Jr., "Beyond Toleration: Toward a New Christian Theology of Religions," *Progressive Christianity*, published by Mobilization for the Human Family, Claremont, CA 91711, Winter 2002, pp. 1, 6-8.
74. John Shelby Spong, *A New Christianity for a New World: Why Traditional Faith Is Dying & How a New Faith Is Being Born* (San Francisco: HarperSanFrancisco, 2001), pp. 180-182.

BECOMING WORLD CHRISTIANS

75. Deuteronomy 5:6.
76. Deuteronomy 4:19-20.
77. William Sloane Coffin, *A Passion for the Possible: A Message to U.S. Churches* (Louisville, KY: John Knox Press, 1993), p. 25.
78. John C. Danforth, cited by Warren Hoge, "U.N. Envoy Seeks to Enlist the Clergy to Ease Conflicts", *The New York Times*, September 13, 2004, p. A9.
79. Mark Juergensmeyer, *Terror in the Mind of God: The Global Rise of Religious*

Violence, updated edition (Berkeley, CA: University of California Press, 2000), p. 146.

80. Coffin, op. cit., p. 24.

WHAT THE MUSLIM SAW IN THE MONASTERY

81. John W. Kiser, *The Monks of Tibhirine: Faith, Love, and Terror in Algeria* (New York: St. Martin's Griffin, 2002), pp. 134-135.

82. Ibid., pp. 244-246.

83. Jay Cormier, "Connections" (New Hampshire: MediaWorks, 2005), p. 4.

84. Kiser, op. cit., p. 52.

KILLING FOR GOD

85. Reuters, "Words of Clinton and Sadaam Hussein: Fiercely Clashing Views," *The New York Times* "International," September 4, 1996, p. A8.

86. James Newsome, *Texts for Preaching, Year A* (Louisville, KY: Westminster John Knox Press, 1995), p. 472.

87. Rodney Clapp, "Calling the Religious Right to Its Better Self," *Perspectives*, April 1994, p. 12.

88. Romans 13:10.

ONCE TO EVERY MAN AND NATION

89. James Russell Lowell, "Once to Every Man and Nation," vs. 1 and 3, *Poetical Works* (Boston: Houghton, Mifflin Publishers).

90. Isaiah 2:4.

91. Joel 3:10.

92. William Sloane Coffin, *The Heart Is a Little to the Left: Essays on Public Morality* (Hanover: Dartmouth College, University Press of New England, 1999), p. 60.

93. Chris Hedges, *War Is a Force That Gives Us Meaning* (New York: Public Affairs, 2002), p. 3.

94. Abraham Lincoln, "First Inaugural Address."

95. James Russell Lowell, "Once to Every Man and Nation," 1845, v. 1.

96. Harry Emerson Fosdick, "God of Grace and God of Glory," 1930, v. 2.

97. Samuel Smith, "My Country, 'Tis of Thee," 1832, v. 4.

A TRIBUTE TO WILLIAM SLOANE COFFIN IN HIS OWN WORDS

"Make Love Your Aim," Sermon, First Presbyterian Church, New Canaan, CT, January 12, 1997.

"Easter 1984," *Sermons from Riverside*, pamphlet, April 22, 1984, p. l.

"Easter and Forgiveness," *The Living Pulpit*, Vol. 7, No. 1, p. 8, 9.

"Do Not Be Afraid," Sermon, Pilgrim Congregational Church, Lexington, MA, April 11, 2004.

"The Good Samaritan Revisited," Sermon, First Parish Church, Lincoln, NE, October 27, 2002.

"With a Warrior's Conviction, Coffin Affirms Peace in Visit," Yolanda Jones, Idlewild Presbyterian Church, Memphis, TN, February 3, 2003.

"Profile: William Sloane Coffin," Religion & Ethics: Interview by Bob Abernathy, August 27, 2004, Episode #752.

"Modern American Patriot: William Sloane Coffin," Center for Defense Information, Washington, D.C., February 5, 1995.

"Rev. William Sloane Coffin Dies at 81; Fought for Civil Rights and Against a War," *The New York Times* Obituaries, Thursday, April 13, 2006, p. A21.

Yale Alumni Magazine, 1967.

Yale Class of 1968, 35th Reunion, May, 2003.

The Courage to Love, William Sloane Coffin (San Francisco: Harper & Row Pub., 1982).

Living the Truth in a World of Illusions, William Sloane Coffin (San Francisco, Harper & Row Pub., 1985), Ch. 15.

A Passion For The Possible: A Message to U.S. Churches (Louisville: John Knox Press, 1993).

The Heart Is a Little to the Left: Essays on Public Morality, William Sloane Coffin (Dartmouth College, University Press of New England, 1999), pp. 60, 66.

Credo (Louisville: Westminster John Knox Press, 2004), p. 132.

Letters To A Young Doubter (Louisville: Westminster John Knox Press, 2005), pp. 21, 97, 134.

EPILOGUE

98. McGraw, Music and Lyrics for Song: *"Live Like You Were Dying."*

99. Mitch Albom, *Tuesdays with Morrie* (New York: Broadway, 2002).

100. McGraw, op. cit.

101. *"Modeh Ani"*

102. Forrest Church, *Freedom from Fear* (New York: St. Martin's Press, 2004), p. 72.

103. McGraw, op. cit.